CHILLY GENTILLY

The History
And
Stories
Of a Great New Orleans
Neighborhood

By
Al Reisz

This is a self published book
Published by Al Reisz, author and photagrapher

Copyright 2016 by Albert H. Reisz Jr.
ISBN 9781541079762

All Rights Reserved.
Cover photo by author. Photo credits are listed at the end of this book.

DEDICATION

This book is dedicated to all Gentillians both young and old and to the area itself, the one that could lay claim to having Pontchartrain Beach, Lawrences, Ferraras, the Pitt, the Fox, Teddys, Luigi's, Verbenas and the A &G if only for a short while. It's also dedicated to, Earline Riviere Reisz, that stylish woman in a pill-box hat with black netting who loved that house on Pasteur Blvd. to her dying day. She didn't pass away in it but she never stopped thinking about it. No doubt she has convinced God to let her cross the wide neutral ground of Elysian Fields to McKenzies to get her butter milk drops and shoesoles. If you're from here you understand what I speak of.

Table of Contents

Preface	Chilly Gentilly	Page 4
Chapter I	Early History	Page 9
Chapter II	DeSoto & The Old Spanish Trail	Page 16
Chapter III	The Gentilly Ridge	Page 20

STORIES OF GENTILLY

Chapter IV	Naval Air Station & New York Street Canal	Page 30
Chapter V	Movie Theaters of Gentilly	Page 42
Chapter VI	Milneburg Snowball Stand	Page 51
Chapter VII	Betsy Comes To Gentilly	Page 56

PHOTOGRAPHS   69-96

Chapter VIII	The Batt and The Beach	Page 97
Chapter IX	'Yats Can Throw Too	Page 111
Chapter X	"He Has Red Hair"	Page 119
Chapter XI	Gentilly Cuisine	Page 125
Chapter XII	Gentilly Inspired Fiction	
	The Seawall	Page 133
	A Chance To Be Tall	Page 137
	Dwayne Makes Good- A Football Story	Page 140
	or	
	(The Plastic Football Championship of St. Raphael, 1963)	

HISTORIC SITES OF GENTILLY

Chapter I	Spanish Fort	Page 176
Chapter II	Milneburg Light House	Page 182
Chapter III	Lakefront Airport & the Four Winds	Page 188

Epilogue	Page 194
Credits and Picture Credits	Page 195

The side wall of the Gentilly icon, Ferrara Supermarket.

PREFACE

GENTILLY

It is strange to think that someone who is writing about an amusement park or a festival where beads and trinkets are thrown at screaming people might consider himself a historian. It is a bit bizarre that history might just be about a bit of shaved ice with some colored syrup dripped over it or a football game played with a purple and gold colored plastic ball. The fact of the matter is that local history is usually about those things and that taken in a larger context any good story that pretends to be factual and has its roots in the past should be considered historical and therefore, interesting to not only himself but to most other people living or having lived in that certain region. Interesting local history has a universal theme running through it that even people who are living outside the region sometimes find appealing. They may read it and say to themselves that yes… it is like our local eggplant dish or a similar barge came through yesterday and hit our bridge support too or that severe storm that spared the longest living tree. So in this sense, this book is somewhat historical as well as universal.

    To say that the stories in this book are factual accounts would be a mistake but then, of course, we might have to sit down and define historical fact. It would seem to most that the only historical fact to be considered would be a photograph or tape of a certain event but then where does that place the old faded photograph of your great grandfather? It is a fact that the picture exists but then, what of it? The general consensus is that no one cares but you because of its personal nature. However, if we are told this photograph is of a man who saved a battalion during the first world war or was an engineer on the first train to traverse the continent then it becomes historical and therefore interesting to not only ourselves but to most who view it and hear the story. The fact remains that most people have someone in their family that has gone to war or participated in some project that was deemed historical. Our memories of these people are all we have left of them for they are long gone from this earth and a photograph does not tell their story. It is what they handed down that lasts.

    In the end it is true that to trust ones memory of certain people and events to be historically correct would be a mistake. History, we are told, is what a mass of people make it, what they think and feel about it. A historian, after all, just might be someone who lives long enough and has a reasonably good objective memory. So without further ado, we give you snow ball stands and Saturday matinees, hurricanes and the tragedy of an assassinated President.

When someone asks me where I'm from and I tell them Chilly Gentilly they look quizzically at me. They ask "where is that"? "It's a suburb of New Orleans, very near the lake", I tell them, but they still have that perplexed look in their eye. "Why do they call it that", they ask. And that my friend is what this little historical compendium is about. Chilly Gentilly is a suburb of New Orleans and what is written here doesn't tell the complete story or come even close to the story but the words here make an attempt at it. These are local stories of New Orleans, of a certain place in the city and they are stories of the past, the not too distant past, the one that is still alive in the minds of the people who might read this. I believe that's what makes them so interesting. In a century or two when the freshness has evaporated very few will care, or they might be looked upon by a few hardcore local historians anxious to know something about the city during the Baby Boom Era but the vast majority of the human race will probably have their attention elsewhere or at least I think they will; they'll probably have better things to do than listen to someone long gone talk about people and places that no longer exist. It is amazing to think that film and tape only lasts a certain length of time; even the images of JFK's assassination are beginning to fade. The printed word, however, lasts a long, long time; longer than film and it can be renewed over-and-over. Look at Shakespeare's folio, but first, let's look at the suburb of New Orleans known as Chilly Gentilly.

CHILLY GENTILLY

Why Gentilly was tagged with the adjective 'chilly' wasn't much of a mystery for those of us who were born and raised near the wide neutral ground of Elysian Fields Avenue.

All one had to do was drive down Lakeshore Drive in December or January and see that there was absolutely no one walking a dog, jogging on the levees or fishing and crabbing from the seawall. Winter on the Gentilly Lakefront was usually too windy and too cold. Whenever an 'Arctic Express' rolled in from the north, it brought downright frigid temperatures that could burst the pipes of raised homes along the lakefront. In later years the New Orleans Levee Board took to closing Lakeshore Drive because the north wind would whip too much lake water over the wall and into the street causing hazardous driving conditions and creating some impromptu ponds where the brackish water would freeze over. Sometimes there was enough ice to skate across; that is, if one had ice skates to skate with; and ice skates in New Orleans are about as rare as snowfalls are. In the late 1980's the weather people took to saying the lake actually had a warming effect on the city and that was why the temperatures in downtown or uptown New Orleans were always a few degrees higher in the winter than, say, the Northshore of the lake or Slidell. For those of us that lived within walking distance of the lake that explanation, ironically, never held water. Somewhere in a photo file there is a picture taken of the "Fountain of the Four Winds" or the 'naked statues', as we knew them, in front of Lakefront Airport. It depicts beautiful icicles hanging from certain anatomical features that shall not be named. It is an old black-and-white snapshot that shows just how chilly Gentilly could be and has always been for those of us that were born and raised there.

   Now reading this, one might have a tendency to believe that we're actually speaking about a suburb of Minneapolis or Chicago. But the debris of this po'boy is that we are actually referring to the geological soup bowl that is the city of New Orleans. New Orleans, which at one time was mostly reed jungles and cypress swamps veined with bayous and lined by a wide lake on one side and a sinuous, yellow serpent of a river on the other. For those of us that call themselves New Orleanians it's The Crescent City, The Big Easy, Sin City, the King of 'H and H' (for the uninitiated that's Heat and Humidity), of summer mornings where every light pole, every phone line, every oak and every piece of vegetation sags with the dew of 99% humidity, where you can set your watch by the afternoon thunderstorms that release thick plumes of steam rising from the pavement of every street like some gigantic outdoor sauna.

Snow ball fight at the Naked Statues, circa 1958.

'THE OLD GENTILLY ROAD'

ANDRES MOLINARY- 1890. (PUBLIC DOMAIN)

CHAPTER I
EARLY HISTORY
FROM THE INDIANS TO THE DREUX BROTHERS

Andrew Jackson is said to have landed at Fort St. John (aka-Spanish Fort) on December 1, 1814. He came to plan the defense of New Orleans, a vital city and seaport to the fledgling nation of the United States during the War of 1812. After studying the maps of the city and surrounding region he deduced that the British would try to capture it from one of three different directions. One of those routes into the city that Jackson knew would have to be defended in one form or another was what he called, the "Plain of Gentilly". Now the indigenous population at that time might have snickered at his terminology for they knew that what Jackson's 'Plain' was referring to was actually the Gentilly Ridge and the road atop it which bore the same name. On Jackson's map at the time the Gentilly Road was also termed an old Indian trail; which of course, it was. His map had three such trails on it. All three were situated on the high ground of the area and used by the Indians long before Iberville and Bienville landed on the banks of the Mississippi in 1699. In time they would become known as the Gentilly Road, the Metairie Road and the Old River Road.

     To talk about Gentilly becoming a thriving suburb of New Orleans one must go back not only to its origins but to the origins of how this unique terrain was formed and to the first human beings that would come to live and travel through it. Some historians say the origins of Gentilly began with the Dreux brothers, Pierre and Mathurin, who acquired over 170 arpents of land along the Bayous of St. John and Sauvage beginning in 1721, only three years from the founding of the city of New Orleans. They purchased the land because the high ground that it contained was the least likely to flood in an area that would constantly battle water inundations from its very beginnings in 1718 until 2005 when Hurricane Katina's surge knocked over levee walls all over the city. The brothers would build a grand home there in 1727 and work a plantation that stayed in their family for many years. They named their plantation, the road and bayou that ran through it, Gentilly, after their commune in old France. When Bienville came back in 1718 to establish the colony on the river he cut the first cane to clear a path and it's said that Pierre Dreux cut the second. So it was that one of the true founders of Gentilly was also among the original founders of the City of New Orleans.

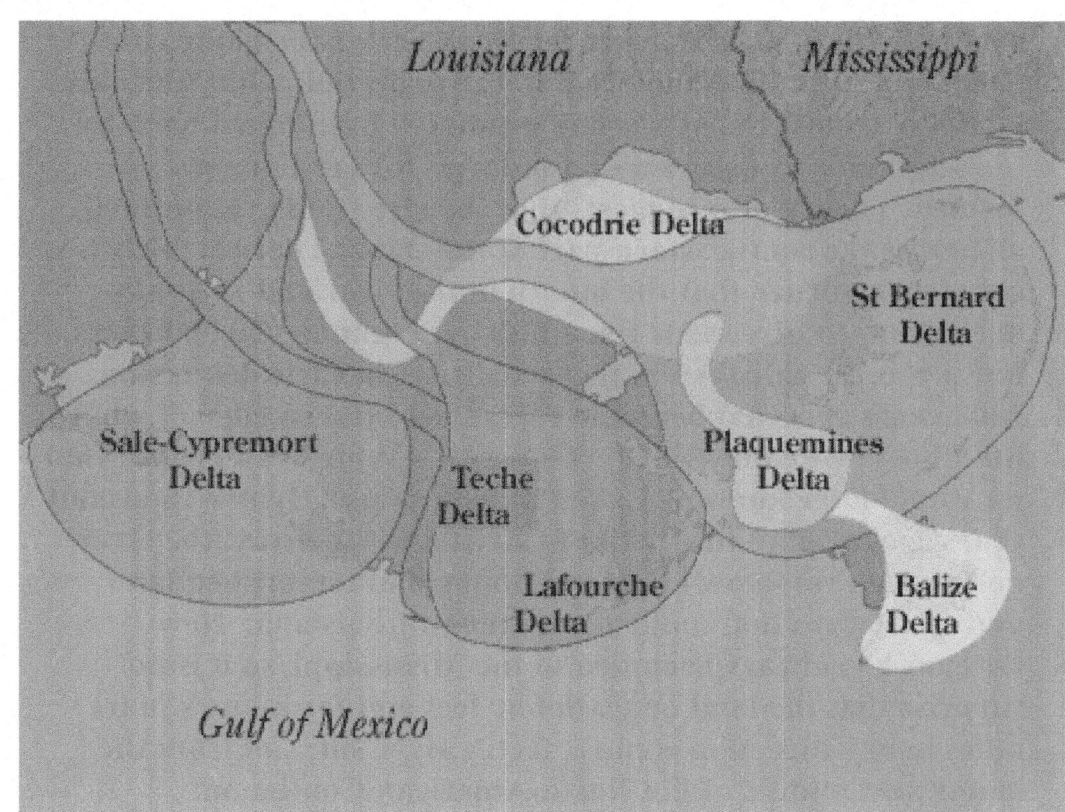

PURPORTED RIVER DELTAS FOR THE MISSISSIPPI RIVER. THE COCODRIE DELTA HELPED FORM LAKE PONTCHARTRAIN SOME 5000 YEARS AGO.

THE TERRAIN

Some archeological geologists suggest that the buildup of the Louisiana and Mississippi shorelines has been occurring over thousands of years because of the outflow of the mighty River. It is also surmised that a few million years ago a large amount of ocean water was tied up in gigantic Arctic and Antarctic glaciers and that the mouth of the Mississippi was actually much further out into the Gulf during the last Ice Age. Over the course of several millennia these glaciers gradually thawed so that sea levels all across the globe rose. 5,000 years ago they had risen to the point that what was once land along most coastlines had gradually been taken back by the seas and oceans as new boundaries for land masses formed. Theory also suggests that the river delta meandered all across the southeastern part of the state. There is fairly concrete evidence that the mouth of the river and its snaky neck changed directions five times over that last 10,000 years; but it was the third delta, the so called, Cocodrie delta, some 3000 years ago, that began to form the southern edge of what the Choctaw People called, "Okwa-ta" (Wide Water) and what we would later know as Lake Pontchartrain. By two thousand years ago, around the birth of Christ a world away, the river delta which we know fairly well today had established land and waterways that make up southeast Louisiana. New Orleans has always been tied to the Mississippi, so it is no surprise that the land beneath our feet and for many square miles in any direction is pure, fertile river silt; soil from the loamy vast middle of the North American Continent.

    Native Americans may have come to the lowlands and waterways of Louisiana some 1500 years ago but there is no certainty as to how long they had been here when De Soto and De La Salle were exploring the New World. It is thought that during the last Ice Age Asiatic Peoples from the Russian Continent may have crossed the Bering Straits by foot and began a slow migration down the North American Continent. It is unclear as to when they arrived and settled in the Lower Mississippi River Basin but we do know that when Iberville and Bienville arrived in 1699 there were several tribes in the Southeast Louisiana area. Among them were the Oumas, later to become the Houmas, the Tangipahoa and the Bayougoulas, all off-shoots of the Choctaw nation. They were firmly entrenched in and around the area as they had discovered ways to cultivate the land and trade amongst themselves and different tribes. They traveled the bayous and lakes and shoreline of the Gulf Coast in dug-out canoes of cypress, a wood they knew resisted the high humidity and excess water that the area became renowned for. For the most part the different tribes lived in harmony with each other but occasionally disputes led to wars that were usually brief but violent. More often than not, though, they lived in peace and would sometimes gather together and hold ceremonies and trade goods. Their villages were usually established near beneficial waterways and grounds that were favorable for cultivation but more importantly, on the high ground that they knew deterred standing water caused by storms and rain.

And, so it was in the Year of Our Lord, 1699, that the brothers, Bienville and Iberville, finally relocated the mouth of the Mississippi River and celebrated a mass there on Shrove Tuesday, (thus, Mardi Gras was celebrated on the day the region was founded). Later they sailed up the river some 100 miles and came ashore at a crescent of land where an Indian village was known to exist amongst the reeds. It had been less than 20 years since De La Salle had seen the mouth of the river and named the land around it, Louisiana, or Louis' Land, in honor of the French King, Louis the XIV. The Indian village the brothers had seen was populated by the Bayougoulas Indians. They were friendly and traded with their new French friends. They also showed the brothers a so-called portage; a well-worn path on which the Indians carried their canoes from the banks of the Mississippi to another waterway, a bayou which their Indian guide explained would lead them to another large body of water that in turn would take them back to the Mississippi Gulf Coast and Biloxi from whence they had traveled by barge. The bayou that the Indians had shown Iberville they called "Bayouk Chopic" in honor of the mudfish (crawfish) that flourished along its' banks. The wide body of water they had also referred to was called, "Okwa-ta", which meant wide water. Of course these bodies of water would later become known as Bayou St. Jean, later St. John and Lake Pontchartrain.

      Messieurs Iberville did not think much of this crescent of land where the Indians had established their village of thatched huts set among the insects and heat; his main fear seemed to be his belief that tall ships would get stuck in the riverbank mud of the Mississippi River at this point. He seemed intent on keeping Biloxi as the main location for this settlement but his brother, Bienville, took note of "this beautiful crescent of land and its convenient waterway" that led to a sea-route back to Biloxi and what would later become known as the Mississippi Sound. It was French Marine Minister, Pontchartrain, who decided that Biloxi was far too open to the elements and wanted something closer to the big river that the first European, Henri De Soto, had seen in 1542.

No. 180. A Louisiana Road.

CHAPTER II
DE SOTO AND THE OLD SPANISH TRAIL

Hernando De Soto was the first European to have seen the Mississippi River. The year is reputed to be 1542. De Soto was on a personal mission to obtain gold but he and his Conquistadores who at times were guided by the Indians indigenous to the area found none of the precious yellow metal in the swamps of the lower Gulf Coast. When he and the rest of his Conquistadors moved through the lower Mississippi River basin they tried to enlist Indian tribes to aid in their search, when they refused the Spaniards treated them cruelly. One has to remember that at this time the Spanish Inquisition was in full force in Spain so when De Soto was turned down in his quest he meted out what he considered justifiable punishment as an example to all the tribes that the Conquistadors might encounter along their way. De Soto is credited with discovering the Mississippi River but the truth is that Native Americans had been using the river and its tributaries for centuries; in fact, they showed the river to the Conquistadores. De Soto happened to be the first European of any consequence to have seen the 'Great Yellow Flood'; the term tagged by the Indians for the yellowish hue of the muddy waters. It is said that De Soto contracted a fever and died on the banks of the river after crossing it sometime in 1544. It is also believed that his body was interred somewhere along the shallows near central Mississippi. The Conquistadors never explored land in Louisiana however, after De Soto's death they tried to find a route through Texas back to Mexico but were forced to turn back by the heat and drought. When they reached the river they decided to build rafts and use it to find their way back to the Gulf Coast and their ships. As they traveled down river, through Mississippi and Louisiana they were attacked by Indian tribes who knew of De Soto's cruelty towards tribes who would not help him. Gradually, they made it to the lower Gulf Coast where what was left of De Soto's men decided to abandon this fruitless quest for gold and return to the safe confines of the Mexican Coast from whence they had come. The facts remain, though, that De Soto moved through several states by way of established Indian paths and waterways. These foot-worn paths based on high ground throughout the southeast would become known to many later as the Old Spanish Trails. The early explorers used them to get around not only the Southeast but the Southwest and some historians suggest that at one time these series of trails may have led from St. Augustine Florida and the Atlantic all the way to San Diego and the blue of the Pacific. In the Southwest, Catholic missions and towns were settled along the Trail. In the southeast, the Indians showed their new neighbors, the Spanish and later, the French, ways to traverse the often soggy swamp lands of Southeast Louisiana and the rest of the upper Gulf Coast.

  As development continued to increase, the footpaths became horse trails, then wagon roads and once the 'Iron Horse' was invented the two rails that make up railroads were laid atop or very near to what were the paths that the old Indians traversed; the 'high ground'. After the dawn of the automobile age the roads would eventually be paved and numbered into a State Highway system that would go nationwide during the latter half of the twentieth century. In Louisiana it was Highway 90 that was built over the shadow of the Indians and the early Spanish and French explorers. It snaked its way across the southern tier of states and became the main thoroughfare in most major urban areas throughout the southeast and southwest. Motels and restaurants often times sprang up on the outskirts of these cities and urban crawl started as suburbia began to proliferate beyond the city limits. It became fashionable to live and play away from the city centers where businesses and commercialism had staked its claim. These two-lane, numbered highways held sway until the vast Interstate Highway System of the 60's and 70's took most of the traffic away from them and their use declined. Still, in most cities the outskirts were still developed along them and continue to prosper because of it but vast stretches between towns saw little or no growth and in some cases such serious decline that businesses and people slowly moved away. Such is the case with Rte. 66 and in some cases, Highway 90 itself. But the fact is Highway 90 is still mostly functional today because it is built on the high ground that the Indians once used. There are many places, in fact, where Highway 90 itself is called, 'Old Spanish Trail' and some say that if you look deeply enough and often enough, on nights lit by the moon and stars you just might see an old Indian or Conquistador trudging down its length.

Zero Milestone.

Zero Milestone erected in San Antonio to commemorate the Old Spanish Trail. 1924.

CHAPTER III
THE GENTILLY RIDGE

Early photo of what is reported to be the Elysian Fields Area.

As already has been surmised, that between the river of 'Yellow Flood' and the large 'Okwa-ta' to the north a crescent of land began to form several millenniums ago as a result of the river delta snaking its way around the area and emptying out its treasure of continental silt from the middle of the North American Continent. Between these two bodies of water land began to form and as a result, bayous or inland waterways formed along with them. But storms and the annual Spring thaw from up north caused these inland waterways to swell up until water burst from them flooding the whole area until it became unrecognizable as land but then the edema would shrink and the waters would eventually ebb back towards the lake and river via these bayous. As a result of this geological process reoccurring over the centuries ridges began to form next to the bayous. These stretches of high ground became the natural choice for travel through the area because at most times of the year they were dry. The Indians used them and when the Europeans arrived they were shown these routes and of course, one of these results became known as the 'Old Spanish Trail'.

    Two of these natural ridges became known for the bayous next to them and would be termed the Metairie Ridge and Gentilly Ridge. There is some speculation that at one time the two bayous actually merged with Bayou St. John in the region of what became known as Allards Plantation, then later, City Park. Some of the earliest maps of the area seem to indicate this but they were very crude and as such not very accurate. One of the better maps does show Metairie Bayou converging with St. John in the aforementioned area; it, however, doesn't show Gentilly Bayou meeting up with its sister waterway. We know this to be true because it was only in the last century that Bayou Metairie was actually damned up from reaching its parent, Bayou St. John. We also know that Gentilly Bayou is actually Bayou Sauvage on the early maps and that it wasn't until the mid- 1700's that it's moniker changed because of the Dreux Brothers naming their plantation after their commune in old France. The Gentilly Road became the main route to and from the city from the east while Metairie Road was used from the West. Both roads are still in existence today. However, the bayous that bear their names are gone for the most part. Metairie Bayou still exists as the waterway in the front of City Park in New Orleans. It's length is vastly reduced but the fact that this remnant of the ancient Bayou is still there is remarkable in the sense that it along with Bayou St. John are permanent reminders of the terrain that was here when the Bayou Goula Indians showed Iberville and Bienville their portage from the bank of the Mississippi to the end of St. John. Gentilly Bayou, which has already been noted, was the original Bayou Sauvage may have been damned up in the mid-19th century as a result of the Louisiana legislature's enactment of the New Orleans Draining Company. Bonded from 1835 through 1868 it was charged with the tasks, to drain, fill and improve all land settled between the lake and the river. The maps of the late 19th century show Bayou Sauvage in Eastern New Orleans but Gentilly Bayou no longer is present on any of them. In present day, Bayou Sauvage still exists in small stretches along Chef Highway in East New Orleans but appears close to extinction as there is no active water-supply to keep it from disappearing during the sometimes hot, dry months of summer. However, the Bayou Sauvage National Wildlife Area, which can never be developed or built upon, still has sections of the ancient waterway as its southern boundary and runs parallel to Highway 90, aka- Chef Menteur Hwy, aka- the Old Spanish Trail, aka, the Old Indian Trail. Seeing this Bayou in existence today is akin to how it must have appeared when the Indians were using the footpaths on the ridge and the bayou water to paddle out to Lake Pontchartrain and the Mississippi Sound.

A Timeline of Relevant Discoveries/Developments pertinent to Gentilly and Southeast LA.

1. In 1542 Henri De Soto discovers the Mississippi River as part of his expeditions in search of gold for personal gain. De Soto and his Conquistadors were led by Indian guides who took them through the Southeastern United States by Indian paths and waterways. It is believed that De Soto saw the river from what would become the middle of the state of Mississippi. De Soto never saw the mouth or the origin of the mighty river.
2. For 150 years no European bothered with the mouth of the river or the Gulf Coast until De La Salle in 1682 traveled not by ship into the Gulf of Mexico but instead by canoes downward from the Great Lakes to finally reach the delta of the river and claim it for France. He named it 'Louisiana or Louis' Land' in honor of The Sun King, King Louis XIV of France. It is believed that De Ls Salle may have been the first to dream of creating a metropolis at the first high ground above the river's mouth. Louisiana was to be ignored no longer.

Historical Oddity: it seems that the river was not kind to the first Europeans or foreigners that espied her. De Soto contracted a fever soon after crossing the river in 1542. He died and is rumored to have been buried on its banks somewhere in middle Mississippi. De la Salle discovered the mouth of the river in 1682 and was soon murdered in a mutiny by his men that same year.

Historical notions: a few notions that are not accepted as fact but are believed by some historians to be a possibility. The priest, Menard, may have wandered from the marshes of Wisconsin all the way down into Louisiana. This purportedly to have taken place sometime in the 1600's with no firm date given. Joliet and Father Marquette did descend the river some nine years before De La Salle but may not have reached Louisiana or the river's mouth before returning northward.

3. The French maritime minister, Pontchartrain, commissions brothers, Iberville and Bienville to 'relocate the almost forgotten mouth of the River Mississippi and establish a colony somewhere in the region that would demonstrate to the world the French occupancy.' The brothers set out from Brest with a small fleet in October of 1698. Sometime in late December they anchored in Biloxi Bay and were told by the natives there that the River lay a short distance away to the west. They set out with their men and two barges and a few canoes and began to follow the coastline westward in February of 1699. The brothers rediscover the mouth of the river on Shrove Tuesday and celebrate mass. They are shown a crescent of land further upriver by the Bayou Goula Indians and are also shown Bayou St. John.
4. A wooden palisade is established by French traders at the mouth of Bayou St. John in 1704.
5. Bienville returns and cuts the first cane to clear ground for the city of New Orleans in 1718. City named for the ruling regent, the Duke of Orleans. Pierre Dreux is a member of Bienville's company.
6. 1721, the Dreux Brothers, Pierre and Mathurin buy 127 arpents of land where they would build their plantation in 1727. The plantation land paralleled a ridge and its accompanying bayou. The ridge was an old Indian path and was the only raised land to the east between the Mississippi River and Lake Pontchartrain. They named the bayou, the ridge and the path, Gentilly. Grace King, the historian, said the two brothers were seldom seen separately. They constructed a grand home with ample rooms, fine galleries and beautiful gardens. The brothers became known as the "Sieurs de Gentilly". The brothers eventually married and had

children. Mathurin's grand-daughter married Louisiana governor, Jacques Phillipe Villere in 1784. In the 1700's the Dreux brothers plantation engaged in the business of cutting timber, raising cattle and brick manufacturing. In fact, the brickyard was still in operation in 1796 when Xavier Celestin Delfau de Pontalba bought 10,000 bricks to aid in the building of the French Quarter establishments bearing the Pontalba name. In 1924, St. James Street, running from Elysian Fields to Peoples Avenue was renamed Dreux Avenue in honor of the 'Sieurs de Gentilly'. A bit of semantics, the word, Gentilly, means in a gentle or noble manner, frankly. It seems that Geoffrye Chaucer used it as an adjective in his 'Canterbury Tales'.

7. France governed the new colony until 1763 when it was ceded to Spain.

8. Spain cedes Louisiana back to France on November 30th, 1803 after 40 years of rule.

9. France sells the territory of Louisiana to the United States for fifth teen million dollars on December 20th, 1803. The sale takes place in the Cabildo, presently the Louisiana State Museum at the north end of Jackson Square.

10. Alexander Milne, a Scottish immigrant and successful businessman in New Orleans buys twenty two miles of Lake Pontchartrain shoreline stretching from Jefferson Parish to the Rigolets in the early 1800's. Milne creates the first artificial harbor on the lake, Port Pontchartrain, and in 1831 the Pontchartrain Railroad, aka- The Smokey Mary, begins operation carrying inner city dwellers out to Milneburg; a collection of restaurants and bars and bathing houses that cater to the public seeking cool lake breezes in the heat of summer. Milneburg becomes a resort area for the city and for nearly a century struggles to exist after several hurricanes wipe out buildings and homes. It leaves behind a small white lighthouse on the banks of the lake and a legacy that might include some of the earliest jazz musicians. Jelly Roll Morton

and a young Louis Armstrong mixed notes with the waves of Lake Pontchartrain.

11. In 1835 it is reported that subdivisions were laid out in the area of Dercantel Plantation which was on Sauniac land in the area of what would become Gentilly Blvd. and Franklin Avenue. It is said that Dercantel himself got a railroad station built at Elysian Fields so that a line could be constructed out to this area. The only information that exists concerning Dercantel Plantation is in a few obscure legal documents. No real description of Dercantel or Sauniac exists.

12. A map of 1849 depicts the Gentilly Ridge as being covered with trees including, Sweet Gum, Pecan, Cincapin and Nyssa Sidiatica. Bayou Gentilly isn't on the map; instead it is named Bayou Sauvage which is the original bayou that the Indians used. North and south of the Gentilly Road and east of Elysian Fields is a plantation called Hopkins Plantation. No description of it or its owners exists.

13. Gentilly begins to take on a less untouched look when some areas are drained and filled as a result of the New Orleans Draining Company enacted by the state legislature and in existence from 1835- 1868.

14. In 1909, developers Michael Baccich, Edward E. Lafaye and R. E. Edgar deMontluzin establish the Gentilly Terrace Land Company. The developers take advantage of the natural high ground and begin building some of the earliest examples of Southern style California Bungalows, English cottages and Spanish revival type homes seen in the New Orleans metro area. The plots of ground were spacious with added fill and set back homes that were a departure from the predominately street-side buildings of New Orleans and most inner cities. A school is built for the new suburbanites that come and shops begin the flourish in an area that had been mostly agricultural for 150 years. Land and houses were developed in Gentilly Terrace until the early 1950's. It would eventually be included in the National Historic Neighborhoods register.

15. In 1918 construction of the Industrial Canal begins. Its first usage would come in 1923. Cost is upwards of 14 million dollars. It brings further development on the eastern side of Gentilly.

16. In 1920 the Catholic Diocese of New Orleans creates the Parish of St. James Major. The first church is resurrected on Gentilly Blvd. close to St. Roch and Spain streets.

17. In 1921 the Milneburg chapel is built at the foot of Elysian Fields. It will serve the people of Milneburg and eventually the personnel of the Naval Air Station built during WWII.

18. 1939-1945, World War II turns the Gentilly Lakefront into a military landscape. The Naval Air Station at Elysian Fields and Lakeshore Drive trains naval air pilots to land and take off from carriers. The American Standard Plant at Franklin Ave. and Lakeshore Drive manufactures PBY aircraft that numbered in the hundreds. A German POW camp is set up across the street where eventually UNO's east campus would be developed. Andrew Jackson Higgins tests his famous boats in Lake Pontchartrain off the seawall very close to this area. President Dwight D. Eisenhower once said of Higgins, "that he was the man that won the war for us". Contrary to some notions Higgins factory was not on the Lakefront but was in fact, very near City Park in the area that would become Delgado College. The immediate post-war years ushered in the Baby Boom generation and brought unprecedented growth to all areas of Gentilly.

19. In the late 1940's, St. Raphael Parish was created and a church built near the intersection of Prentiss and Elysian Fields Avenue. A newer church and school was built later during the 1950's.

20. By the 1960's most of the land in Gentilly had been fully developed and it becomes one of New Orleans most populated and busiest suburbs. The area teems with life; schools, shops and businesses abound.

21. By the 1970's the apex of growth is reached and a slow decline began as development begins full force in Jefferson Parish to the west. Lower land and housing costs were the main attractions for those that wanted to escape what they sensed was becoming over-taxation and an aging infrastructure.

Present Day:

After the devastation of Hurricane Katrina in 2005 Gentilly once again began to take on the look of an undeveloped suburb. Houses, businesses and schools, all of which were swamped for over a week were systematically demolished as time wore on in the once popular suburb. Vacant lots with open views that hadn't been seen since the early part of the 20th century greeted those who had been born and raised there. The one glaring exception to this change to open space was the continued deterioration of the infrastructure; mainly the city streets and their sewer covers that rise up like volcanoes in the middle of some thoroughfares. One must maneuver around them very slowly and carefully or face the demise of countless automobile front ends and suspensions. Some of the main avenues have been re-paved but the many side streets, all, are a sad commentary on the city's maintenance of its infrastructure. The sad truth is that the city of New Orleans has rarely been kind to businesses in the way of taxation and with the outdated holdover of Huey Longs, "every man has his castle" homestead exemption that creates a joke of legitimate property taxes, the city coffers see very limited tax revenues. What little does accumulate is spread much too thin to go around and as a result leaves the outer edges of the city on the lower end of the maintenance priority list. The other sad constant in Gentilly, as it is in most other neighborhoods, is the fact of ground subsidence in the urban 'soup bowl' that is the terrain of the city of New Orleans. The land between Gentilly Blvd. and the lakefront was described in early maps as reed jungles and swamps. As it was developed in later years only Gentilly Terrace which lay mostly on the high ground of the Gentilly Ridge was filled and raised up to accommodate the new homes. Most of the other sections of Gentilly were mostly drained and sparse fill used to grade out the lots prior to development. An original inhabitant of the area once said that these areas were drained and filled with what he described as coffee grounds left over from the French Quarter; he wasn't the first to describe the soil in Gentilly as of 'coffee ground consistency'. These swaths of underfilled lots were the first areas that saw the land literally begin sinking right beneath our feet. Those houses in Gentilly that had cast cement steps leading to the front doors were at first comprised of three or four treads but after 20 to 30 years of existence another one or two had to be added as the ground began sinking below them. In photographs of the area you will see fire hydrants rise up a yard or two above the level of the street. It makes for an odd, yet very appropriate image that is all 'Chilly Gentilly' and New Orleans.

Fire hydrant and ground subsidence.
Marigny and Pressburg Street. 2015.

THE STORIES OF GENTILLY

CHAPTER IV
The Naval Air Station
And
The New York Street Canal

The Naval Air Station and London Avenue Canal, 1948.

    As children, snotty noses and all, colds are worse during the summer. It is an oxymoron to have a cold when tar bubbles up from between the sheets of concrete that made up our street. Growing up we didn't have the slightest idea how the area we lived in began. We kind of thought, but not really, that the Pitt Theater had always been there and that God had set Ferraras Supermarket down at the corner of Elysian and Robert E. Lee; set it down with the idea that it not ever be moved or relocated and certainly he did that for Lawrence's Bakery at Filmore and Elysian Fields, home of the best hot glaze and cream donuts around. The Red Velvet cake and doberge squares were to die for. How these places got there was no mystery to us; they had always been there and always would. Oh, the naïveté of youth! Later, though, say around 12 or 13, I began to take a vague interest in the origins of our neighborhood and the area surrounding it.

    At the end of our street, on one of the corners of Pasteur Blvd. and Robert E. Lee lived Mr. Nichols, an old guy who was forever building a large wooden boat in his back yard. It seemed that every neighborhood, from Gentilly to Carrolton, to the By Water had an old guy like Mr. Nichols building a large wooden boat in the back yard. Why was that? Mr. Nichols was missing the right thumb and forefinger on his left hand. I don't remember if he actually told us how it happened but an accident with a chain saw or circular saw comes to mind. I do remember his telling us that our neighborhood was built on 'coffee grounds' and that years ago it was nothing but swamp and wetlands and the only thing out this way was the beach area at the end of Elysian Fields and that a train had run down it for many years, long before it was actually paved. I don't believe we ever completely understood why he used the term 'coffee grounds'. Was it because the area was filled with some sort of dredged material or simply because the ground beneath us was sandy or grainy? In any case, Mr. Nichols claimed to have picked cotton grown in fields that were now our streets. As kids we were always aware of cotton having some influence in our past lives but we had never seen a cotton plant as kids. Gentilly was a strictly urban environment. It wasn't until I was in my early twenties that I first saw a cotton field and that was in a small Mississippi rural town. Mr. Nichols, God rest his soul, never lived long enough to see his boat launched. However, he did finish it with the help of a son who, after his father passed away, put the final coat of paint on it and moved it to the Lakefront Marina. The rumor was that it floated beautifully for two or three days after which, the son and his family came out one morning to take it out on the lake but found it on the bottom of the marina. It seems that the wood dry-rotted beneath all those coats of paint that the old man was constantly brushing over it. He did this to protect his project from the 99% humidity that Gentilly and New Orleans is renowned for. Sadly he, like so many others, had taken too long to finish the job. Thankfully, he wasn't alive to see it.

One only has to look at the width of Elysian Fields Avenue to see that at one stage of its history that it would have accommodated a set of train tracks quite well. The neutral ground on Elysian Fields had to be as wide or at least the same size of the neutral ground on Canal Street downtown. Elysian, though, was a much prettier expanse of ground with its palm trees, (many of which survived Hurricane Betsy in '65) and its thick palmetto bushes. The ground was wide enough for us to have many a pickup football game on and its well-manicured grass was lush enough to even play 'tackle' on. The neutral ground was maybe too wide for some. I can recall more than a few people cursing its width during the hottest days of the summer while running to try and catch the bus or having to wait for the traffic lights to change so they could try and cross it.

The train as most people know was the Smoky Mary. It ran for nearly a century from the 1830's to the 1920's and it took the hot and sweaty people from the Quarter and downtown to a resort area known as Milneburg after the Scottish immigrant, Alexander Milne, who bought up acres of beachfront property from Jefferson Parish to the Rigolets. He established the first port of call on the lake, Port

Pontchartrain, and around it a collection of camps and houses sprung up that catered to the city-bound with restaurants and bath houses. Milneburg, it is said, may have contributed to the birth of jazz. We do know that Jelly Roll Morton played there and so did a young Louis Armstrong.

It may have been that in the late 1890's and early part of the 20th century that houses began to spring up some distance from the actual resort area of Milneburg. This seems to have occurred between New York Street and Robert E. Lee Blvd. (aka Hibernia St. and Edinburgh St.) bounded by Elysian Fields and St. Roch Avenue because this area came to be known as Milneburg on city maps and some of the houses there date back to the early 20th century. On the southern end of this development we know that the Gentilly Terrace neighborhood was being planned and built from 1911 on. Started first between Elysian Fields and Franklin Avenue bounded by Gentilly Blvd. and eventually Filmore Avenue; these two early housing developments began a slow merge towards one another.

A friend of mine purchased one of the buffer houses, very near the corner of Filmore and Franklin Avenues. I was helping him to renovate it when one day we ventured up in the attic to do some electrical work. What we found up there was a window into the past. It seems, back in those days, when one had to add more room to an existing structure they simply built around the old one. The attic area was an old bedroom and part of a kitchen from the early Jazz Age. It appeared that when construction started they just sealed this section off and left everything in it as it was. It was like rummaging through a living museum or being transported back in time seven decades. We had a glimpse into the lives of the people that lived there nearly 80 years ago.

He and I sat for a few hours reading copies of the Times Picayune and States Item from the mid-1920's. I had seen copies of the Norman Rockwell covers of the Saturday

Evening Post; well, he and I went through the original magazines from that era and marveled how well-preserved some of them were. They were fresh and soft like they had just been delivered to the door of the covered front porch. Was that the plop we just heard as it hit the screen door and slid to the cement below? Stuck between some of the floor joists were some toys from a young child's collection; there were also pots and pans used in the kitchen. He and I sat there rummaging through the remnants of a family that in all likelihood was gone from this earth. As we sat, the sunlight from the small octagonal window at the front of the house faded and we knew that the people who had once been here had seen that same light. We sensed that they had been there all along waiting for us to discover this so they could exist once again through us even if it was just for a short while. As dusk emerged, before evening, we saw and heard the development of the neighborhood through the decades. It was a natural, normal progression that as one looks back seemed perfectly logical. The building that went here, the store that went there, that certain open lot that became a ball field, the cemetery at the end of the street.... All came to be because it was meant to be. It went just how the urban planners believed it would go. It followed their plans. When we at last re-entered the world below we were groggy from the past, it was if we had walked through a thin veil that separated one room from another and as the veil slid softly past our vision we blinked at the speed through which eighty something years had passed. It was no wonder our legs were wobbly and that we felt like we needed a roast beef on French and a Dixie from Teddy's Grill across Franklin Avenue.

    As progress comes to pass certain city projects reached completion. The enclosure of drainage ditches and their complete invisibility to the residents is something that the city of New Orleans has always strived for. As the tax base expands and money fills the municipal coffers this will occur.

It did in our neighborhoods, much to the chagrin of the kids and young adults who aren't yet old enough to have forgotten about the New York Street Canal.

The playground of all playgrounds of our youth was the New York Street Canal. It now lies buried under a good portion of Leon C. Simon Blvd. and the last remnant of New York Street itself. To our parents it was undoubtedly an eyesore but those of us that grew up in the shadow of its ten or so blocks we saw many fun-filled days along its banks. We'd never forget the day the last bit of earth was bulldozed over it; water came welling back up and with it some shiny minnows, some crayfish and a box turtle that crawled over the wet but now quickly drying mud.

The canal ran along the full length of New York Street; from Elysian Fields Avenue to the Greater London Avenue Canal. The actual water stream at the bottom of the canal was very meager except during those summer rain storms when the stream could become a rushing torrent of water that could easily take human life. It was not unusual to find a car down one of its steep banks after a Saturday night partying but most of us were well aware of its existence and the danger that it could pose during rain events.

We took part in a great many activities around its steep banks. Chief among them were the great many army battles that ran along both sides and was witness to the din of all sorts of plastic weaponry. On the far bank was a fence that ran along the Naval Air Field and was usually obscured because of a twenty yard strip of ground that all sorts of vegetation grew upon during spring and summer; especially summer when it would become so dense that is was easy to lose your squadron if one ventured more than a few feet from them during a mission. It was ideal for scouting missions where if one knew the terrain well enough he could hide himself among the jungle weeds and ferns so as not to be seen by the enemy as they read their comic books and planned their next move. This jungle on the far side was also a good hiding place to be utilized when either parent needed something done and was on the prowl for a son or daughter to perform it. Yes, girls back then had some spunk too. There were more than a few who were unafraid of the snakes and rats that lived along its banks. Of course there were some who never ventured far from their manicured front lawns and never knew what they were missing.

Most of us learned how to or how not to fish in the mysterious steam of water that ran down at the bottom of the canal. Which bait to use was always a subject of conversation. The most popular seemed to be Sunbeam white bread. You were supposed to take a little bit of it and ball it up with your fingers and somehow get it to adhere to the barb of the hook. It just seemed that whenever this good idea hit the water it inevitably fell off and the minnows close by would immediately go into a feeding frenzy and whisk it away from our make-shift rods and reels. One longed to hook something very large in the canal but the best I can recall, the largest fish to be caught may have been the length of an index finger. However, there was that time when we were fishing near the middle of Cameron and New York when all of a sudden we saw this huge wake coming towards us, it looked like a huge monster slapping water on both sides of the canal as it erratically swam straight at us. It scared us so bad that we threw our poles down right where we stood and lit out for home. Later that day we learned how old man Thibodeaux had released a three foot sand shark into the canal after his weekend fishing jaunt out by Lakefront Airport. We had our chance to catch something big and we blew it.

At the end of Saint Anthony Street another canal ran into our canal. This waterway, though, had been covered over years before the New York Street canal and the only thing now visible of it was its cavernous cement opening that was some ten yards across and as mysterious as the pitch blackness that enveloped it. We would lean precariously over the side and yell into its mouth to hear the loud echo of our voices come back. Also in the region of our canal was the black pipe.

The black pipe was a water supply line that was about 12 inches in diameter that emerged out of the bank on one side and was carried by a wooden trestle some 10 feet in the air over the canal where it would disappear back into the bank on the other side. To us kids, it represented the ultimate challenge that the New York Street canal had to offer and that challenge was crossing over that pipe by foot. For us, only the bravest or very foolish were able to traverse it. This was no small feat to accomplish. The wooden trestle seemed quite high and if one ventured too far from either side they were faced with a dangerous fall that I'm sure caused grief for more than a few parents of the children who fell and broke or badly sprained arms and legs attempting to cross it. Of course, with us kids, it became a badge of honor to have 'made it'. You really didn't belong until you had made the walk over the pipe. It was a focal point for the neighborhoods that surrounded the canal. The brashest of teenagers would casually walk across it while swigging from a bottle of Dixie; the youngest of us were always seen scooting across it on their backsides, just waiting for the day when they too could be considered 'cool'. The pipe is now buried deep below the road bed of Leon C. Simon Drive. It may not be visible to the human eye but to the initiated it is still there, shiny and black and still calling to us.

There are a few personal remembrances that should be related about our dream field, the canal. But apologies must be issued. First, to the future environmentalists, for we were too young to realize that those concoctions we made in the garage that contained just about every household chemical and garden pesticide we could find would cause all those minnows and perch to go belly up in the water after only a day or two. I'm not too clear on exactly what we were trying to do but I feel we were not intentionally causing anything or anyone undue harm. I must apologize to Teddy for leaving him all alone on his front porch when his mom answered the door that day to find him covered in quick- mud from neck to toe. He was still in his Sunday best following morning mass at St. Raphael. I know I said I would stay with you and help explain but the moment that the doorknob turned I just about pissed my pants knowing how your momma being a good Italian woman and all had the uncanny ability to string foreign sounding phrases together at very high decibels. I seem to remember the slap of a leather belt as well and have always felt extreme guilt whenever it has crossed my mind. Lastly, this is not an apology as much as it is a statement of forgiveness that goes out to my long deceased father. For I know if you were here you would earnestly apologize for taking my worn, tattered and foul smelling, 'Smoky the Bear' teddy bear and burning him in one of those weekend trash fires that frequently took place on the banks of the canal. I know he was old and full of holes and that you were teaching me a lesson on life; namely, if you took better care of your toys I wouldn't have to incinerate them. Just kidding, dad, don't think I've ever forgiven you for it.

    The other constant of our childhood in the 1950's was the presence of the Naval Air Base that sprang up during the military buildup on the Lake Pontchartrain lakefront before and during the World War II. The base occupied all of the land that is now the University of New Orleans main campus. For the longest time it was surrounded by a tall chain-link fence with barbed wire atop it. It formed the northern boundary of the canal on New York Street and as kids we would press our faces to the fence and watch the planes and jets come skidding in.

    When LSUNO was first established in the late 1950's the college had no choice but to use as classrooms those old wooden framed buildings from the WW II era. I can recall wandering through those structures as a kid and recognizing something very old about the smells and atmospheres that enveloped them. The only structures left from the base are the tall, brick smokestack near the lake, an old airplane hangar and the small security building that was probably one of the original guardhouses to the base. There was also in this area a relatively small bomb shelter that was erected in case the Germans decided to attack the base during the war. Most people don't believe me when I tell them that UNO had a shelter but it's true and it was not an atomic bomb shelter like the ones that were buried deep underground and lined with concrete and steel. It resembled an oversized walk-in freezer that simply had dirt pushed around and atop it and there were a few vents sticking up from the mini-summit of its small hill. Its main features were the two massive steel doors that opened into its meager square footage. It, also, was an eerie sort of place when one was inside of it.

    The bases runways paralleled New York Street and ran for nearly a mile. A mile might have been perfect for the prop planes of the WW II but were sorely inadequate for the jet planes of the 1950's. That is probably one of the very real reasons why the military gave up the land to the local and state governments; it could no longer use the runways safely. As a young boy I can recall the sonic boom rattling the dishes in the cupboards and windows of the house while some of those early jets were being flown overhead. We also distinctly recall the sirens of the firetrucks from the base and the city racing onto Elysian Fields Avenue when yet another jet had run out of runway and crashed through the fencing and onto the street. It must have been quite a frightening thought for a pilot coming in for a landing over the London Avenue Canal knowing that he was going to run out of runway and hoping he could throttle back in time before he would make the turn at Elysian Fields Avenue. It didn't take long for the naval authorities to figure it out; the air strips were dangerous and could not be used.

For a while its buildings stood empty. Before the university got rolling we would slip through the tall fencing and walk the runways that were now hidden by the creeping grass and weeds of neglect. Later, they bulldozed the runways and created dolmen-like structures that we would play in and under for a while. They became caves and fortresses for our imaginations to feed on. Thank God our parents did not know what was going on after we slipped through that fence. If one of those broken slabs of concrete would have fallen we would not only have been interred but crushed as well and they probably wouldn't have found us for a long time; at least until the huge shards were trucked out of there. As a child you pass some tests early on in life. Some you have no knowledge of until much later, usually not until adulthood when you say to yourself, 'wow, were we ever fortunate that that didn't happen, we must have been crazy to do such a thing.'

    A few months later the last remnants of the runways were removed and yet another tangible symbol of our childhood and the WW II era was gone. Although most of us Baby Boomers were born after the war, we were still keenly aware that it played a major part in our existence. As children we played army games and no one wanted to be the bad guys, the Krauts with the square helmets. Some of the comic books were still about the war and just to the east of the airfield was a large army base that was also no longer being used. Camp Leroy Johnson was rendered mostly defunct after the armistice was signed. Today the University of New Orleans east campus is housed there. On the extreme east corner of this land is the reserve bases for a few branches of the armed services; this is the last vestiges of the WW II era on the shores of Lake Pontchartrain. What we did sense about the war was an immense gathering together of not only men and women for the cause but the ability to garner land and resources that this country of ours is renowned for. This has to be a fairly frightening aspect for any country that finds itself on the foe list of the government and people of the USA. This makes the Vietnamese War especially puzzling for a lot of people; especially veterans of WW II whom did not know or accept the word, 'defeat'. What we came to realize later is that not only were the Viet Cong being aided by the Chinese and Soviet governments but that our own military was tying the hands of its soldiers with incompetence and petty differences between the services. The full might and power that was displayed during WW II might never be seen again. Not only has ideas and people changed but the advent of the nuclear age has rewritten the strategies that encompass war. Now there are no set rules, we are walking on egg-shells, hoping desperately that those countries that possess nuclear capabilities also possess a clear understanding that to use such a weapon in anger or frustration might doom us all.

The Jefferson Davis Avenue Canal being "boxed" in. Circa- late 1940's- 1950's.

CHAPTER V
THE MOVIE THEATERS
OF GENTILLY

In the late 1950's and early 60's if one wanted to go to the movies in Gentilly there were actually three choices of movie houses. First, was the Gentilly Orleans, a movie house which was in a sort of strange location; right next to the Peoples Avenue Canal on Gentilly Blvd. right by the train overpass. Dropping kids off at this location was difficult for the parents because one had either to go down Gentilly Blvd. and make a hazardous U-turn which took forever because it was such a busy street or go behind the theater and come up the other way by the canal. There was always a line of cars, usually irate mothers trying to either drop their kids off or pick them up for the matinees. I suspect these difficulties were the main reasons why the Gentilly Orleans wasn't very popular with the parents which in turn meant low attendance figures. To my recollection it closed and reopened more than a few times and, I believe, even took a few stints at becoming an art film cinema, somewhat like the Prytania Theater off of Carrolton Avenue but it finally transmutated into an ordinary drug store and never showed movies again.

Still, it was a strange theater, dark with sconces on the walls covered by artificial ferns of some sort. It was a smallish cinema but had a very large balcony which overshadowed the down section. Too many times we were forced to sit up in the balcony and when you are ten you want to be close to the action on the screen. Those that sat up in the balcony were usually looking for 'action' of another kind. I will say this that it showed a few movies that stuck with me through the years. One was a B horror film by the name of 'The Tingler' which was an eerie film about a centipede like creature that could attach to your spinal column and actually frighten you to death; the other was a surreal horror flick titled, 'The Mask' which took you to a place where horrible creatures roamed around in gondolas on canals.

The other theater in Gentilly was the Fox. It was near the northeast corner of Elysian Fields and Gentilly Blvd across the street from the Jewish cemetery and sandwiched between a fire house and a gas station. The Bell super market was on the southeast corner directly across the street. The thing I remember most about the Fox were the enormous velvet drapes that hung in the lobby. It seemed as if they stretched fifth teen feet or more from floor to ceiling. The lobby itself was tiny and the entrance to the theater was guarded by black swinging doors that had thick smoked glass panels in them. I don't remember the Fox having Saturday matinees for us kids; consequently it was always labeled as an adult's theater, a place that our parents probably went to.

This brings us to the Pitt Theater. There was nothing finer than spending a Saturday afternoon at the Pitt watching the short comedy films of The Three Stooges followed by a Vincent Price movie like 'The Pit and the Pendulum' or an Elvis flick like 'Kid Galahad'. The Pitt was the place for us. It took up the northeast corner of Elysian Fields and Hibernia Street, which later would become Robert E. Lee Blvd. It was a large rectangular building with a glass enclosed ticket kiosk out front. The sign on top of the building took up a good portion of the façade on the southern end of the building. It was done in beautiful neon tubing that spelled out the name of the theater in chaining lights. The parking lot was huge, at first covered with just clam shells from the shores of Lake Pontchartrain but later asphalted over. The size of the lot made it a favorite of parents who often times came with their kids to see the movies. There were glass enclosed billboards in front that advertised the coming features and many a kid could be seen staring up at them while their big brother or sister waited in line to get tickets. The building was large enough to have another business concern situated there. In the nineteen fifties it was Parkers Drug Store which had an olde time soda fountain and grill in it. Our first malts were bought there and the hamburgers were fresh and juicy with crisp French fries. It also had a huge candy counter with the large glass bowls filled with one and five cent varieties. It eventually closed in the 1960's and was empty for a while but then a restaurant, Taco Tico, took over the space and had a long run as one of the few Mexican restaurants that did well in Gentilly.

    The Pitt had four pairs of double doors right next to the kiosk. One set was used for entering the theater and the other for exiting after the show was over. As you entered, immediately to your left was the refreshment counter with its ubiquitous popcorn popper filling the lobby with its buttery smell; also the glass candy counter where you could buy anything from Milk Duds to Sno- Caps. Around the perimeter of the lobby were more glass enclosed billboards announcing coming features. On the far wall across from the entrance doors were the Boys and Girls restrooms. Above the stall in the Boys restroom was an exhaust fan that was constantly turning and making noise and one could always see daylight through its louvers. That was the only daylight we saw until four hours later when the matinees ended. Coming out of the theater it was a jolt to our eyesight after coming out of the dark into bright sunshine. We squinted most of the way home or until our eyes adjusted.

    After entering the lobby the main body of the theater was to the left of the restrooms. You reached it by walking up a wide set of steps that ended at a long partition wall that was painted a dark blue. It was this wall that prevented the screen from being seen by anyone standing in the lobby and also kept out any indirect light. As you ascended these stairs and reached the partition the balcony section was immediately above and behind you; actually situated over the main lobby area. There were right and left stairways that led up to the balcony as well as access to the lower seating areas. The balcony, though, was usually the main purview of the older kids. One had to have reasons to be in the balcony and chief among them was a girlfriend or boyfriend to sit up there with. It was a mature sort of place, mysterious to those of us that were too young to have a reason to be up there but later we figured out why there were so many dark seats up in the balcony.

The walls of the main viewing area were softly lit by art deco-like sconces. I'm sure there are a few people around, including myself, who would love to have saved one for a memento. The main aisle carpets were some swirl-like design that was done in brown and white, very similar to the color of the neon lighting on the façade. The only times we saw these rugs clearly were when the exit doors situated on either side of the screen were flung open after the features which allowed the afternoon sun to stretch down the aisles of the theater. The cement slab in between the seats was almost always slick with spilled soft drink resin and smashed candies of every type and description. Even with tennis shoes on you had to be careful of slipping and depositing your bottom or more residue upon the floor. The smell of buttered popcorn was everywhere; even the people there early before the popper was fired up could smell it cold from the night before.

During the performance one was likely to be hit in the head with a Milk Dud thrown by ones enemies, or a stray, flat popcorn box thrown Frisbee-like might catch a shoulder blade. Most of the time we were fairly well behaved, intent more on what was on the screen than what was below it. Occasionally, though, we'd be viewing a film that couldn't hold our interest and then the proverbial 'hell' would break loose. Management would then break in with a sort of 'time-out' and stop the picture until we had calmed down. This, thankfully, didn't happen often.

Being as young as we were, we generally didn't attend the matinee with a girlfriend or boyfriend. Sometimes to feel a little older than we were we we'd take a girl with us or meet up with one in the lobby and go up into the balcony seats. We found out early just how painful it was to keep your arm around a girl for four hours. It was a badge of honor with us boys just to see if we could leave it there for the first hour or so. Not many of us made it that long. Most of the time, though, we sat there with our buddies and talked about what we were going to do later or what had gone on that week. There was not enough time to discuss everything before or during the movies, so our time there wasn't for catching up on anything but the latest films that Hollywood had to offer and most seemed to be made for our generation, the Baby Boomers. Most of them were extremely wholesome and moral but they were some of the corniest fables ever made. It was a forgone conclusion that the good guys were going to win. However, even if there was no clear-cut victory for either side the fable always implied that somewhere down the line the bad guys would be punished and the good finally get the girl, the man and their just rewards. The truth was that compassion for ones enemies was very rarely shown but when it was it made a lasting impression on us. At the Pitt we saw just about every Elvis film that was made. We loved Elvis because he was the epitome of cool; he was the king of non-statement. You messed with him and you either got beat up or sung to, one or the other. It was no mistake that back then our social strata had an element of guys that dressed, talked and looked like Elvis. The girls in this group usually teased their hair high on their heads, wore white blouses and black, tight-fitting pants. These were the daredevils of our world, they were the guys with a woman on their arm and a pack of cigarettes rolled up in the sleeve of their white t-shirts. They were also the guys who personified the rebel, they were the ones dropping out of school too early, getting married too young and starting a family too soon. They were known to us as the 'hoods' and we yearned to be as cool as them.

We also saw the best of the Japanese made monster films; Godzilla, Rodan, Morthra. Who can ever forget Morthra being hoisted high above Godzilla on the wings of Rodan in order to save toy Tokyo and its obvious, fake Japanese army from certain destruction? Back then there was no mercy for Godzilla, he was always considered the bad guy, and as such had to meet his end, preferably before the movie ended and if not then, certainly it was implied as he walked out into an inevitable, watery grave. Tokyo saved yet again. The terrible truth about those movies was that you had to give something up in order to save the world. This was the martyr complex; someone or something had to lose their life. Rodan was a martyr and hundreds of thousands of those way too many Japanese civilians and military personnel were martyrs to the fable. We always believed that less population in Japan was a good thing, at least that's the way it was portrayed in their films. It seems that like, Darwin, they believed in the process of natural or should I say, un-natural de-selection.

The horror films back then were mostly moral as well. We grew up watching Vincent Price meet his inevitable end in a multitude of ways. We gasped at his cruelty in 'House on Haunted Hill', we shrieked at his ugliness in 'Masque of the Red Death' and we marveled at his madness as the giant, guillotine-like pendulum swung over a puzzled Jack Nicholson, his brother-in-law in the 'Pit and the Pendulum'. The traditional horror films (The Werewolf, Frankenstein and Dracula) were already in existence so Hollywood started its famous regurgitation machine and re-made them all again. Christopher Lee and Peter Cushing made us cringe with fear in the Dracula series. Our imaginations were spurred by the death scene when Christopher Lee finally meets his end and turns to dust and bone as sunlight flooded into the chamber where he was impaled with the stake. We saw Michael Landon sprout excess hair and fangs in 'I was a Teen Age Werewolf' and we felt compassion and sorrow for his demise although we knew he could not and would not escape his sad fate. We saw back then the first signs of the fantastic evolution of special effects in the movies that future films would heavily rely on. In 'War of the Worlds' we watched as the Martians' machines defied not only gravity but every weapon known to man including the atomic bomb. It was the first time we heard the term, "force field", but it seemed to make perfect sense. We would see it used from then on in almost every sci-fi film made. We were captivated and charmed by 'The Time Machine' and its scenes of time unrolling before us as the machine accelerated faster and faster. Much later, when we were grown, we discovered that this film won an Oscar for Special Effects and weren't surprised by it because we knew it to be that good. It was a neat film. We went home the day we saw it believing that time travel might be possible. We played in our backyards making time machines out of cardboard boxes and rusted gym sets. It was also one of the films that stirred our passions. We knew why Rod Taylor was going to leave behind modern civilization and return to the beautiful Weena and help the naïve Eloi. We could see by that film that love was possible and that it was good, that it was a going to be a positive influence on our lives.

    We managed to see some skin in the bikini movies made with Annette Funicello and Frankie Avalon. They are so tame by today's standards that even the bikinis are as laughable as the dialogue. We were always shown just enough that our imaginations didn't have to work hard to figure out the rest. Seeing a woman dance in the sand or a man for that matter dressed, it seemed, only in their underclothes, was wild (which is why the term was used so much in the titles of the movies). On a personal note, I fell in love with Annette before the bikini movies from her days on the little screen as a regular on the Mouseketeers shows. Her face and smile seemed perfect to me. I have to confess to sitting through one of her movies, 'Babes in Toyland', seven times; and most of those viewings were from the balcony of the Pitt. I felt closer to her up there. Annette, wherever you are, I remember and my heart always has a place for you.

One little known fact about the matinees back then is that sometimes the management of the Pitt would hire local talent to perform on stage before the features began. These were usually local clowns or magicians who obviously were not used to such a big stage and therefore, never left a lasting impression on kids waiting to see Elvis or Vincent Price. They were never booed off the stage, although they at times heard an occasional impolite comment or noise. They were not on for long, though, and were probably happy to see the first few frames illuminate the screen behind them.

As we got older the matinees grew fewer-and-fewer. After some years they stopped all together. The single screen movie theater was being replaced by cinema-plexes with multi screens; so the Pitt tried keeping up with the times by breaking up the main theater into three or four screens. There are now very few of the original neighborhood cinemas in existence in any city. The ones that survived were usually the grand movie palaces that dominated the downtown urban areas during the Great Silent Era of films but places like the Pitt and Gentilly Orleans have long since been plowed under. A Walgreens Drug Store now stands in place of the Pitt at Elysian and Robert E. Lee; its shelves stocked full of sundries that now occupy space where the laughter of thousands of children echo. Its polished and waxed tiles overlay the carpets and slick slab of a generation ago. Something stirs in the heart, though, when walking through that store, something moves the soul when viewing that corner from afar. On dark summer nights it might be a figment of my imagination but I could swear there are times when I not only see the chaining neon of that marquee but can hear the hiss of the gas. If you close your eyes long enough you might just see some kids looking up at a glass enclosed billboard to see what's playing next.

The Pitt Theater on the northeast corner of Elysian Fields Avenue and Robert E. Lee Blvd. Circa- early 1950's.

CHAPTER VI
THE MILNEBURG SNOWBALL STAND

To children in Minnesota a snowball is something you make with your hands during the winter and throw at your friends. To kids in New Orleans a snowball is something you buy in 95 degree heat to eat and cool off. The children of the 1950's and '60's didn't know that a thing called air conditioning even existed. We had seen the strange looking boxes hanging from windows, making noises, it seemed, forever and always a stream of water dripping from it that kept the flowers beds below moist. These were the first room air conditioners that were used and for the longest time we didn't know what they were and really could have cared less; we still played outside and found ways to entertain ourselves in the heat of Gentilly summers. One of the finer things of our lives back then was cooling off with a snowball soaked with spearmint or cherry syrup; but chocolate seemed to be everybody's favorite because the bottle was almost always empty late in the day. So you see, about the only thing a snowball made in Minnesota has in common with the Louisiana variety is that they are both cold. Other than that they are a world apart.

Our snowball stand was in a strategic location; literally just paces outside the Pitt theaters exit doors. Actually, it was a small white shed on the side of a Milneburg house at the corner of Elysian Fields and New Mexico Street. The house was an old one with a high, wide porch with lights. It was one of those New Orleans homes that had stairs ascending to the porch of the main house with a sort of basement area underneath where you could store all that useless stuff or do as most people did, use it to park ones car or cars underneath. The stand usually opened late in the day and kept churning for most of the evening. On really hot days and nights it was a gold mine for those who owned it; you had to stand in line just to get your hands on that paper cone with the cool elixir in it and fork over your nickel. For a nickel you got a small paper cone with shaved ice and syrup on top. At that cheap price one was always never enough. We'd have four sometimes five in a row because they were so addicting. We always left with sticky hands and faces from the sugary syrup.

    We also were familiar with the ice houses of the day. They were the size of small buildings and often in store parking lots. They had a small porch in front that one walked up to and deposited a quarter or two into and have a chunk of ice the size of a cinder block come sliding out. We often wondered whether these ice houses were automated of did they have someone directly behind the coin slot waiting to slide the ice out. We found it difficult to believe that they were fully automated back in those days. For years there was one in the parking lot next to Ferrara's grocery store. Ferrara's Supermarket will always be fondly remembered as the only store that opened and gave food away during the aftermath of Hurricane Betsy. We walked in ankle deep water down the aisles and picked out our favorite items. It was a strange, eerie sight being in there wading through the water with no lights on. The ice machines were not used by us so much as they were by our parents who utilized them for barbeques and fishing trips. What is remembered, though, is that back then there were no plastic bags of cubed ice. One had to buy this large chunk and then get an ice pick to chop it up into smaller pieces. This was almost always something your father did. The sound of an ice pick pecking away at that block was a familiar one and it usually meant good food and cold drinks were soon to follow.

    Another facet of the snowball stand that amazed us as kids was the actual machine that made the ice into snow. This rather large block of ice seemed to be put into a mini oven with an iron door that locked with a large handle. A switch like a wall switch was then flipped on and a loud machine sound could be heard. Another long handle was then grasped with one hand while the other held the paper cone cup with a metal funnel over the top so that when the handle was turned, shaved ice would enter through the funnel and shape the snowball. The complete process didn't take long except for when the block of ice ran out and the operator would have to stop and open up the machine to place another block next to the cutter blades. The syrups that were poured over the ice was usually kept, it seemed, in old whiskey bottles on shelves above and to the side of the machine. On the outside of the stand was a large wooden sign that had all the flavors listed in acrylic colors. The bottles were also tagged with little printed signs for the flavors. When the cone cup had been filled and shaped with pure white ice, the operator would then ask which flavor was requested. He would then take the bottle and hold it upside down over the ice and as the liquid came trickling out would move the spout in a circular motion from the outside of the cup to the inside but always being careful to not let the syrup drip over the sides. When he reached the middle he would usually let a good long trickle come from the bottle to make sure that the syrup reached the bottom. But not always, as this last flourish was the operator's prerogative as he had the power of time and taste on his side. For the people he knew it meant a syrupy snowball; for those he didn't care for it meant seeing white ice at the bottom of the cup. After the syrup was poured a straw and small wooden spoon was thrust into the finished product and handed over to the customer. Paper napkins were always given and one could tell the popularity of a certain stand by the amount of napkins and stained paper cones littering the grounds surrounding it.

  In the early mornings the stand had an eerie quality about it. One could see the remnants of activity and the absence of customers from a place that attracted them the day before was all too obvious. Something always felt missing from there in the early mornings with the litter and the bees buzzing around the trash cans. The wooden flap over the serving window announced the stand was 'CLOSED', and that sweet, sugary odor simmered from the day before. As the present day went on the feeling about the place would evaporate as activity picked up but in the morning it was a place we'd rather not be; we always felt something unseen was lurking there, something that frightened us just a bit.

    Of course snowball stands have persisted to the present day. There are some, like the one uptown on Plum Street that have survived from the past and have done it with timing and ingenuity. The Plum St. stand did it by creating snowballs with flavors that were combinations of other flavors and also with added toppings like evaporated cream and scoops of ice cream or even adding ice cream products like malts and sundaes to its menu. Other stands soon followed suit and some survive but the vast majority of the old neighborhood stands have long since closed. Gone are the days when the landscape surrounding a stand consisted of a few wooden picnic tables dominated by mostly trash barrels and litter. The stands of today sometimes have wooden decks with comfortable tables and chairs and beach umbrellas to shade its patrons. It's now the standard to comfortably sit in the shade and eat ones snowball while watching the traffic and life go by.

    On a personal note I would like to deny the five cent snowball eating record that some have attributed to me. While it is true that I downed six five cent chocolate snowballs in one sitting; I vehemently deny that it was eleven or twelve as some have said. As it with most things in life, time has a way of playing with the truth, stretching it and distorting the facts. Besides, I'm positive that on that particular day I had only thirty five cents in my pocket. Maybe.

Milneberg House, much like the one on the corner of New Mexico Street and Elysian Fields Avenue where the snowball stand stood for many years.

CHAPTER VII
BETSY COMES TO GENTILLY

As a child one usually doesn't notice weather unless, of course, it is snow which is such a rare sight in this part of the world that even a kid has to notice. The change of seasons in New Orleans (which usually means from heat one day to cold the next) basically goes unnoticed by most kids. Their attention span is focused on whom the next ball is to be thrown to, what friend should I play with now because I'm mad at her for what she said yesterday to that other friend; but I didn't hear it myself so it must be true, and so on and etc..... Kids are focused on other kids and not what time the sun rises or sets. Does it really have a certain time it does that? However, there are certain weather words that catch kids attention spans quickly. One, which we already know, is snow; the other is *hurricane.* That is a word that gets almost all kids juices flowing. All kinds of mental images go to work in their active imaginations, they see huge torrents of water running through their streets, they hear loud winds whistling through their homes and their faces pressed to the screens of open windows as large trees are uprooted and carried away by titanic winds. To a large extent, those images can be reality in a hurricane. The sad truth is those images are frightening to most adults where most children feel excitement at the thought of them Most children do not see their safety in jeopardy at the mere mention of the word.

In the 1950's and early 1960's the word hurricane didn't mean a whole lot. We didn't have the information that people have today, there was no Weather Channel, no Learning Channel, no Discovery Channel; no cable television of any sort. As children we had no real conception of what a hurricane was; we had never really seen one and what it caused was a question mark to us. We could plainly see, though, that the word caused a mysterious feeling to emerge in the adult world and that feeling passed on to us. We wondered what all the fuss was about; why were people boarding up windows, why were they moving their cars around, why were some leaving home with suitcases and bags packed. Yes, we wondered what all the fuss was about.

Before weather satellites were launched in the late 1960's and early '70s, hurricanes were usually tracked by observations from other sources which usually consisted of ship reports and plane observations out at sea. It is unbelievable now that most people prior to this time were almost completely unaware that they were in the path of a hurricane. One has a crazy mental image of some meteorologist taking pressure readings while the town is falling down around him right about the time the eye of the storm is over them to finally confirm that, "yes, it is a hurricane" that has hit them. In that context it is not hard to understand that many people lost their lives in those early days of weather watching.

Hurricane Flossy was a storm like that. It was a category 1 storm that hit the city on September 24th, 1956 and most people were unaware of its path. There was no advance notice given. Fifth teen people lost their lives in this storm which caused 25 million dollars in damage. Our recollection of it as very small children is not very strong. I do recall sitting up at a window most of the night and hearing strange sounds caused by the wind gusts. At daybreak we awoke to a sight we had never encountered before; the street and front yards were all covered with water. The New York Street Canal had overflowed its banks as the pumps could not keep up with the amount of rain water that came with Flossy. She dropped fifth teen plus inches of water on the city. We immediately went outside in the front yard and played in it; a colossal mistake, we learned later in life because that water had the potential to carry several diseases that could have made us all very sick. However, at the time, we had never seen such a thing; it was novel to us and something for our imaginations to seize upon. There is an old photograph somewhere of us kids using a garbage can as a boat in the front yard and splashing about in the water. In the end, Hurricane Flossy was just a ripple in the historical pond that would grow larger in the next decade.

By September of 1965 hurricanes were not only tracked from outer space but were flown into by airplanes sent out from the Hurricane Center in Miami, Florida. At this time the storms were still given feminine names. That practice was finally halted in the 1970's after the women's movement complained about it being sexist. Afterwards, the storms were given co-ed names. In the first week of September of that year our parents had been watching a storm named Betsy come up through the Caribbean and scoot up the eastern coast of Florida where it appeared to take aim at the Eastern Seaboard of the United States. Steering currents that year were not very strong so it may have surprised a lot of people that Betsy did a complete loop and turned right around like a spinning top on the linoleum of a kitchen floor. As it crossed over the southern tip of Florida and emerged in the southeast Gulf of Mexico it drew a bead on the southeast coast of Louisiana. As it did so people began hoping that it would spin away but the closer it came to the coastline the more hope began to fade until resignation finally set in that it was going to hit us.

This was the first storm that we made preparations for as a family. All loose items outside were put away, some of the windows in the house were taped up. The cars were put in the back of the driveway on the highest ground the property had to offer. We made trips to Ferraras and the hardware store to buy candles in case the power was to go out. We bought containers to put water in and filled the two bathtubs with clean water. We had batteries for the flashlights and transistor radios. Then we waited.

What was unusual about Betsy was that as it approached the city it became obvious that it would hit us during the daylight hours. As young kids we had been brushed by tropical cyclones before but they always seemed to come during the night when we couldn't see what was going on outside our windows; we began to believe that hurricanes only came after dark but Betsy drew near right after the dawn. Betsy was soon to shatter this childish assumption and many more before it was done.

At 10:00 AM on Friday, September 10, 1965 we began to notice the effects of Betsy. The pine and crepe myrtles in our front yard were beginning to bend over toward the ground. All of the trees in the neighborhood were in full motion, their crowns were being pushed around like the hair of boys and girls on a March day when the winds blow hard during pre-spring in New Orleans. We had seen strong wind gusts before but they had always abated, whatever damage they did was over within a few seconds. We saw that these winds were not going to be as brief.

They grew stronger and a howl began that would fill our ears for what seemed like hours. We sat by our windows and couldn't believe what we were seeing. The neighbor's house across the street had a clay shingle roof that began to unfold in the wind. We watched in amazement as whole rows of roofing tiles began to peel off and become deadly missiles in this wind. We saw them hit and embed themselves into trees and telephone poles. When they hit automobiles they shattered and fell, harmlessly, to the ground. We saw large tree limbs being pushed down the sidewalks and the middle of the street. Most trees either fell to the ground or began to break apart in the winds. The ones that were strong of limb and trunk didn't fall or break but every bud and leaf was stripped from it as if it were in winter. The amount of familiar debris that came by was amazing. We saw pieces of signs from all the stores we knew; the grocery, the gas station, the barbers, the hardware. All their advertising had finally reached home only it wasn't there for very long and we were lucky to be able to decipher what little of it we actually did see.

There was plenty of rain associated with Betsy but it was mostly the stinging variety that fell in sheets and didn't really accumulate in our streets. As such, the New Your Street Canal did not overflow its banks and flood the neighborhood. The pumps held their own until the power went out and by then the storm's precipitation was well over with.

Our dad, who was one of the classic fire-engine chasers you hear about, decided that he wanted to take a drive in the car while Betsy was dancing outside. We jumped at the chance to see the destruction from a different angle but as he backed the car out of the driveway we began to wonder if this was such a good idea as limbs and debris began to pelt the car like shrapnel. At the middle of the day all was gray and everything was shuttered but the awnings of buildings and houses were either completely gone or hanging by a few leftover pieces. Most commercial signage was beat up or gone, whole sections of buildings were exposed and their insulation and tar paper flapping in the wind; it was a botched operation that had gone wrong. Those telephone and light poles that hadn't gone down were leaning over at precarious angles. The lush, tall palm trees on the neutral ground of Elysian Fields had taken a severe beating. Their root balls being small and shallow meant they were at a disadvantage in the wind and many of them simply went down. As kids we loved to play around and under them and to see them this way made us realize that our lives were going to be changed by this storm. When our dad saw sparks shooting off in the road from a downed transformer he knew that it was time to head for home. When we arrived back the power was out and we wouldn't see electric light for at least a week.

Morning became mid-afternoon quickly and as it did the wind and rain died down. By then a lot of people began to emerge from their homes to view the war-like landscape that had been thrown over the neighborhood. Much later we began to realize the similarities between war bombardments and hurricane aftermaths with the amount of debris and destruction that was left behind. We felt like war victims only we were hurricane survivors but we shared in common the disruption of everyday life and the chance misfortune of having our homes severely damaged or reduced to ruins. For some of us Betsy was a violator, a miscreant with a temper and the ability to change lives. By early evening it was over and the quiet, the silence following it was somewhat deafening.

After the first hour or two of surveying their damages, people began to act. We heard chain saws being revved up as downed trees were no doubt being cleared away. A multitude of hidden trash cans reappeared and kids were sent into yards to begin picking up all the debris that was deposited there. The sound of portable radios could be heard but it wasn't music we were hearing. It was a local news station that told us the latest news, directing us to do certain things, warning us not to do certain others. Life was beginning to stir but it was not returning to normal. We would discover later just how abnormal life would become.

At about dusk we realized that the only artificial light we were seeing was that from flashlights and the headlamps of cars. The streetlights did not come on as they usually did, and there was no lamplight behind our windows. In its place one could see the flickering of a multitude of candles. It was an eerie sight and made us think about when the lights went off during harsh thunderstorms. That first night was flush with the odors of food. People started pulling meats and fish from their freezers and lighting up their grills. Neighbors kept offering us plates of food, bowls of tepid ice cream, anything that was refrigerated or perishable was now on the menu. What wasn't would be in the garbage by tomorrow.

Early September in New Orleans can be almost identical to early August. In fact, it is not unusual for all of that month to see temperatures in the 90's with the ineluctable humidity that everyone in this part of the world knows and loves so well. When Betsy took the power that first day the adults of the neighborhood looked on it with great trepidation while we kids saw it as a chance to have some fun like an immense camp-out that everyone would have to go on and maybe last for a more than just a day or two. But after that first day and a half, everyone grew sweaty and dirty; we were always told to take a bath and now that we wanted and needed to take one, we couldn't. The mosquitoes saw easy pickings and descended down upon us, their human feast. We soon tired of eating just meat, there were few vegetables being grilled, most people freeze steaks and chops they catch on sale at Schwegmanns first and ears of corn or packages of lima beans or okra second. The amount of food being tossed from dead refrigerators was astounding if not downright repugnant. It was weird to think that people would have to shop all over again once the power did come back on but no one, nary a soul knew when that would be.

Listening to the news on the radio we learned that Betsy had not just gone quietly upstate. Her legacy lived on through the storm surge it brought into the lake and pressure it brought to bear on the levee system that encircled the city. When we awoke the next day there was a foot of water on our street. We saw a white trout swimming in our back yard. Surely the rain brought in by the storm had not caused this; it would have happened almost immediately if that was the case. No, we learned that a section of levee along the vast Industrial Canal in Eastern Gentilly Woods had been breached and water from Lake Pontchartrain was now flowing westward from the Industrial Canal to the Peoples Avenue Canal and eventually down the streets of Gentilly. At Franklin Avenue and Robert E. Lee it was close to four feet deep but by the time it reached Elysian Fields and Robert E. Lee it had slowed to twelve inches or less and there was nothing the authorities could do about it but stand there and watch. It must have been a real sinking feeling they experienced with now an average of two feet or more covering their city.

Of course, we kids saw this as another opportunity to play and the adults would have to come along for the ride or endure our bored expressions around them for most of the day and night. You could see from the expression on their tired faces that they were beginning to lose patience that the power was out. Life had become too exhausting for them. They definitely felt like victims. We took to splashing in the foot of water that covered the street. On the way down we talked about the storm and the power it displayed, we screamed about all the destruction that we had witnessed. We walked to the corner of Pasteur and Robert E. Lee and stood on the neutral ground and looked out over what had now become Lake Gentilly, partner to Lake Pontchartrain. It was an eerie sight to look straight down Robert E. Lee in the direction of Franklin Avenue and see nothing but the shimmer of water surrounding half-sunken cars. While we stood shoulder-to-shoulder there on the neutral ground we sensed that this was going to be one of those moments in time, we innately felt this was a sight we'd never forget nor see again; at least not in our lifetimes.

We trudged down to the commercial corner of Elysian and Robert E. Lee and saw waves lapping at the sides of Ferrara's Supermarket. We walked around to the front of the building and peered into the windows to see water residing between the shelves and counters. We began to wonder just exactly what they were going to do with all those wet baseball cards and gum. Across the street the Pitt Theater stood alone in its large parking lot, rising out of the water like a mountain all on its own. We could see the flood water grew deeper the further east one went. A few big-wheeled military trucks slowly went by. They were carrying members of the National Guard; they had been called up because of what was now an emergency situation. They warned people through loudspeakers that they should stay close to their homes and out of the flooded streets. We were somewhat incredulous to hear from these guys that someone had drowned in the streets close by. We could see that maybe the deepest part of the flood waters might be around five feet at the most. We scoffed and frowned at them; but our know-it-all expressions soon dropped to sheepish resignation when they quickly explained to us that the man-hole covers for the sewers had been lifted off by the pressure of the mounting flood. When the pressure equalized what you were left with was a hole in the street that couldn't be seen with the naked eye. It seemed someone had been walking around with their friends just like we were now doing and had fallen into one of the holes and been swept away underground. We saw the seriousness in the guards' eyes and turned around to head for home. This time we stuck to the neutral grounds to be sure to avoid any open manholes but even then we walked gingerly and planted our feet with some hesitation.

  By the following day the flood waters were gone. Blue skies pervaded the rest of the week and things slowly went back to normal. The power, which had been off since the day of the storm came back on a week and a day later just when everyone in the area was getting somewhat used to living without it. While it was off our homes began to slowly go back to the way New Orleans must have smelled pre-electricity and pre-air-conditioning; always an odor of dampness and humidity. Betsy, however, added another element when the flood waters hit our streets and the underneath sides of our homes; the area took on an added odor of something from beneath the sea. It was like being near the beach in a cottage.

But that too disappeared within a day or two of the power being restored. The windows and blinds were closed, few people were seen outside but it was when our television sets were switched back on that we began to see just how devastating a storm Betsy had been. It had been especially cruel to those in lower St. Bernard Parish and for those who lived anywhere east of the Industrial Canal where the levee systems were severely breached by the surge that rolled in through the Mississippi River Gulf Outlet Canal. It was there in the Ninth Ward of New Orleans that members of some families drowned in their attics trying to escape the rising water. It was after this storm that authorities advised people to place an ax in their attics just in case they had to chop their way out to escape. We learned that some people had evacuated to the high-rise hotels downtown only to see freighters rise up near the foot of Canal Street as the surge flowed up the river from the Gulf. It seemed the Crescent City was in peril not just from the surge entering Lake Pontchartrain but also from a swollen Mississippi River; this twin threat floods the area frequently but was created as well by draining the swamplands and extending shorelines further into the lake. This caused land subsidence and created the so-called 'soup bowl effect' that urban experts now say puts our city New Orleans at grave risk. In a 'perfect storm' scenario a hurricane coming directly up the mouth of the river would first dump lake water into the city and then 10-15 feet of river water. That would fill the bowl up with possibly no way to get it out of the city for at least several days or weeks. This image played havoc with people's minds so that post-Betsy long range flood prevention measures were implemented. These consisted of shoring up the levee system, raising it and extending it. That work continues even now.

    Betsy's legacy lives on in many ways. It seems that the winds of the storm picked up seeds of an especially destructive vine species as it tore through the Caribbean and deposited them down in the City of New Orleans. This vine grew rapidly and extensively and it tentacles began to smother all that it clung to. Some of the old oaks in the area which survived a hundred years or more were killed off by the 'hurricane vine'. Its root system was so deeply buried that one had to dig deep to even have a chance at eradicating it from our gardens and even our parks. On a personal note; after it had killed a cypress tree that we bought for our mother one Mother's Day I decided that it was time to wage war against it. I got out into the garden that abuts the driveway and dug and pulled on it until I was sure I had all of it captured. For added measure I scorched the earth it had been thriving in with gasoline and let the flames die just as I hoped the vine would eventually do. After a few weeks I was elated to see that there were no shoots poking through the loam where it had been. I went about my life conducting my business with no thought about the vine clouding my mind. A few months later while walking down the driveway, while reading some college text; I looked slowly to my right to see the vine again creeping from the earth, its tentacles reaching toward anything it could grab a hold of. I realized instantly that my folly was in thinking I could beat it, that I could totally rid our soil of it by pulling only a few hundred strands of its root system and scorching the earth from whence it sprung. I knew now it had reached underneath the cement slab of our driveway and was just lurking until the danger had passed so it could rear its ugly, destructive tentacles on the other side. I made it my mission that year to continue to wage war against it. Whenever I saw newborn shoots poking through the soil I'd start pulling on them trying to get as many of them as I could. In time my persistence paid off and I eventually eradicated it from our yard. It gave up its hold on us and color again thrived in our yard but its presence elsewhere in the neighborhood was pervasive; the backyard trees of the house directly across the street were covered in it and I could see it every time I walked out the front door, reminding me that I needed to stay vigilant myself but even now, almost half a century later I still scan the landscape for it and cringe whenever I see it covering a tree like an umbrella or a blanket used by a smotherer.

  A decade later my father decided that it was time to have the exterior of the house re-painted. We were sitting in the den watching television one afternoon when one of the painters knocked on the back door and spoke a few sentences to my dad. He walked outside with the painter and was standing near one of the back windows pointing up at the wooden casing surrounding the window. My sister and I walked outside to see what they were conversing about. We saw them point to three pieces of tile that were embedded in the wood like they had been peeled from a deck of cards. We knew immediately that those bits of tiles were driven into the wood by the force of Betsy's winds. We recalled how we watched as they unfolded off the roofs of the houses across the street and could hear them hit other houses like shrapnel; they were a testament to just how powerful the storm had been. The painter asked dad if he wanted him to remove them. My father looked at those pieces of tiles a moment and said no; leave them. Nature had put them there and there they would stay, a reminder of that day in September of 1965 when our family rode out a storm named, Betsy.

The dreaded 'Hurricane Vine' brought in on the winds of Betsy.
House on Filmore and Elysian Fields intersection.

The Battle of New Orleans hero-
Major General Andrew Jackson. Commemorative medallion.

**Battle of New Orleans Bi-Centennial, January 8th 2015.
Chalmette Battlefield, Chalmette, LA.**

**Ancient Bayous of New Orleans. Remnant of Bayou Metairie.
The front of City Park, New Orleans.**

Ancient Bayous of New Orleans. Bayou St. John near Lake Pontchartrain.

Ancient Bayous of New Orleans. Bayou Sauvage along Chef Hwy. Bayou Sauvage was called Gentilly Bayou near the Dreux Brother's Plantation in the early 1700's.

Historical sign on the banks of Bayou St. John. This is the spot that reportedly is where the Bayou Goula Indians led the Messrs. Bienville and Iberville.

Historic picture of Lake Pontchartrain shoreline. Taken from Milneburg lighthouse, October of 1927.

Milneberg Lighthouse and Restaurant. Taken early 1900's.

Milneberg camps and restaurants, 1927.

Milneberg Lighthouse, 2015.

The Smoky Mary. Steam train that ran from the French Quarter to the Milneberg resort along Elysian Fields Avenue.

Time Table for the Smoky Mary. Early 1900's.

De-stumping Elysian Fields Avenue. Circa- 1935.

Gentilly Streets. Verbena Street, circa- 1929.

**Elysian Fields and Prentiss Avenues, looking east.
The 2nd St. Raphael Church is the elongated white building in the upper right corner. Taken late 1940's or early 1950's.**

Elysian Fields Avenue just prior to the removal of the tracks. Intersection of Elysian Flds. and Good Children Ave. Early 1930's.

Marigny Street and unknown intersection. Circa- 1935.

The intersection of Filmore and Elysian Fields Avenue looking west. The Gentilly icon, Lawrence's Bakery, is on the left. Circa- 1959.

Vermillion Street at the intersection of New Mexico Street. Circa-1950's.

Elysian Fields Avenue is blocked while the New York Street Canal is being boxed and filled in. Circa- early 1960's.

The Gentilly High Rise under construction. Circa- 1965.

The London Avenue Canal. Looking north from Gentilly Road. 1905.

The London Avenue Canal and Naval Air Station. Aerial shot- 1948.

Pontchartrain Park, Press Drive and the Industrial Canal. 1955.

St. Rita's Chapel or what many consider the first St. Raphael Church. Late 1920's or early 1930's.

**The second St. Raphael Church. Prentiss Avenue.
Taken late 1940's early 1950's.**

The third St. Raphael Church. Now called The Transfiguration. Picture taken post Katrina.

St. James Major Church and School. St. James was the first church and school in Gentilly. The present church was finished in 1953. The First St. James Major was near Spain St. and Gentilly Road. No picture or drawing exists.

St. Francis Cabrini Church and School.
Built in 1962 the church and school are now demolished.
Picture was taken 6 weeks after Hurricane Katrina devastated the area.

CHAPTER VIII
THE BATT AND THE BEACH

Pontchartrain Beach's mid-way clown.
This was the clown that could give you nightmares.

As a kid growing up in Chilly Gentilly in the nineteen fifties and sixties there was no better place to be on a summers day or night than riding the rides or walking the mid-way at Pontchartrain Beach. The Beach had grown out of the WPA land reclamation project along the Lake Pontchartrain lakefront area; a result of one of many Great Depression projects begun under the FDR administration. A seawall was erected from the West End of New Orleans to the Industrial Canal in the east. As a result, the old resort area of Milneburg was replaced with new shoreline and so Harry Batt Sr. shuttered the old amusement park at Spanish Fort and opened up the new Pontchartrain Beach at the end of Elysian Fields Avenue in 1939. Batt Senior officially ran the enterprise until

1970 when his two sons, Harry Batt Jr. and John Batt, took over leadership of Playland Amusements Inc. and ran it together until 1983 when the Beach officially closed its gates and left New Orleanians without a real amusement park. For the first time in nearly 200 years New Orleans had no resort area along the lake to which inner city dwellers could go to and enjoy the cool lake breezes that made the long hot summers somewhat bearable. For over 40 years, though, New Orleanians and in particular, Gentillians, had a place to laugh, to be entertained and to be thrilled by the rides and games on the mid-way.

It was erected out on the 'coffee grounds' of old Milneberg and developed into a vast amusement complex that included carnival rides, stage music and in-ground swimming pools built right on the sands of the lake. If you didn't want to feel the sand and shells of the lake bottom you could swim in the chlorinated waters of the concrete pools; there was even a pool built off to the side of the largest in-ground pool in the city that contained high-dive diving boards which became a real badge of courage amongst all us kids. Few braved its heights but those that did came away with a real sense of accomplishment.

In its day the Beach rivaled some of the great amusement parks of the country. The rides were not the traveling carnival variety but were of the latest technology and science. One which was called 'The Wild Maus' was one of the most frightening rides a kid could go on; its track system was built in three tiers, a single car with two seats and mouse ears for hood ornaments would take you high in the sky and jolt you through a seemingly endless series of sharp turns and gravity defying dips until you were breathless and closed-eyed at the end. The whole ride probably took less than five minutes of your time but wow, what a five minutes it was! No great amusement park was complete without a roller coaster and the Beach had a great one; some say the best wooden trestle roller coaster ride in the country. It was called, 'The Zephyr'. And there was always a line of people waiting to get on it. Most of us stood there meandering through the parallel fences that led up to its Art Deco platform with great anticipation. Once in the ten car train, going through the dark tunnel that led up the first steep hill you began to wonder exactly what the hell you were doing there, putting yourself through this torture, this great fun that everybody said it was. As you were ratcheted skywards that distinctive clinking of the motorized chain could be heard as the cars were slowly pulled uphill. Most focused their vision on the red beacon that was atop the wooden spire adorning the hill and signaling that the apex had been reached. As you passed underneath it you knew that a 'g' or two was about to push your stomach back into your spine. What was amazing were the excited screams that came out of everyone's mouths as they were dropped down the first hill. Those screams could be heard in almost every nook and cranny of the park. Someone should have made audio tapes of that motorized chain followed by that pause and then the screams. Someone did have the presence of mind to save that trestle and the light that was atop that first hill. Today, long after the beach closed its turnstiles; it sits in a small grassy park on Williams Blvd. out in Kenner, LA. I've seen adults stand in front of it with their children and go through a whole series of animated gestures while obviously trying to describe to their kids exactly what it felt like to have ridden it. Their kids stand there mystified; most unable to comprehend how a bunch of sticks could bring such excitement to their parents' faces.

    To us kids, the Batts were mythical people. We knew of them but if they were to be standing in front of us we probably wouldn't have known it. I don't recall ever seeing a picture of them or having someone pointed out to us that those people there were the owners of that great place. We knew there was a building by the Penny Arcade that was away from the main strip of the mid-way which was the administration building. We had heard that there was a residence there within it. The building was also done in an Art Deco style consistent with the bath houses built in 1939 and painted a brilliant white, the color of Florida Panhandle sand. Whenever we walked around the Beach at night we would walk by this building and see lights glowing on the second floor and wondered if the great Harry Batt was looking down upon us.

It is a well-known fact to swimmers that one of the ways to escape the dreaded New Orleans, H&H (Heat and Humidity) was to get into the water, any water but if it was an in ground pool, especially one with a deep end, then to swim down to the bottom and enjoy the cool water which was around 65 or 70 degrees. Of course, the bigger the pool meant the more cool water there was to swim through and there was no pool bigger than the in-ground pools at Pontchartrain Beach. It seemed as if it stretched for one full city block in length and was just as wide. For a kid it was an awesome sight.

During the height in popularity at the Beach it was not unusual to find fifty people or more swimming in that pool; people of all ages and sizes were there enjoying the water, the sun and the fact that you were near the action of the Beach was perfect because when you were tired of the pool and all shriveled up from being in the water too long, you could get out, go get dressed and then start your walk down the midway. 'Down the midway' meant for us young dudes, finding a couple of girls that struck our eye and then trailing them all over the place until one of us worked up the nerve to go over and talk to them. Sometimes this process went more slowly than we would have liked, like say ten years or so, and the girls may have come to us first and started their move. This was almost as embarrassing as closing your eyes on the Zephyr.

To swim in the pools one had to bring a towel and their swimming trunks, bathing costume, leotard, kitchen sink or whatever; the point was that you could not swim without a suit and not the coat and tie variety. As you moved through the main entrance to the Beach, past the Zephyr and onto the midway, there stood the Art Deco styled building that was the bath house; in it were the boys and girls dressing rooms. The building itself didn't seem that big until you were inside it. It had brightly colored terrazzo floors throughout with metal drains placed in the floor that collected water from the showers and the locker rooms. It appeared to be ill-lit with high, smallish windows that gave about as much a view as they did light. There were wooden benches to sit on while you changed your clothes. Because the building was mostly stucco, concrete and metal there was a marvelous echo system throughout it. One had the feeling that you were in some cave somewhere underground with sound bouncing off the walls. When you emerged into the sunshine and air a walk of a hundred yards or so lay ahead before you reached the pools. If you hadn't brought sandals with you, you had to hop-scotch your way as quickly as possible because of the heat built up on the cement walk-ways. I can recall groups of kids and adults tip-toe running their way back and forth. It made for great comedy. When you were at the pools you entered through the gate where a person took your token and let you pass through into the fenced off area. The fence was a vertical bar fence that had metal plates cut into the shapes of sea-shells, crabs and fish , painted in bright, pastel colors welded to the side of it. One would walk the length of fence to find an area to place towels and sandals then walk to the edge of the immense pool and sit down to dangle your legs in the water and look out over the sea of screaming kids. In the water there were whole groups of kids talking amongst themselves like they were standing in the middle of the street in their own neighborhoods. If you knew these kids you would go over to them and join the group. Very few people actually swam in the pool, it seemed to be mostly a social gathering place with either people you knew or people you'd like to get to know. Even though there was very little swimming taking place there was always a lot of kicking and splashing going on. The area was inundated with the glee of 'pool sounds'.

Next to the immense, usually over-crowded swimming pool that everyone from the city of New Orleans appeared to be using was the 'high dive' pool in its own separate enclosure. It was probably an eighth of the size of the bigger pool but what it lacked in stature it more than made up for in mystique and that aura was strictly due to the fact that this pool had a very deep end to accommodate legitimate high diving and to us kids fifth teen to twenty feet in a deep end could be terrifying especially if you didn't have a grip on swimming. Plenty of kids were never properly taught how to swim but instead, paddled around or treaded water as if they know how to. Most of the time these 'swimmers' stayed away from the deep end of the pool but occasionally you'd find one or two splashing close to the sides in the deep end with the most terrified expressions on their faces. One could see that they were having no fun negotiating around the deep end. Now you take that kid and throw them into the high dive pool where there was no shallow end and you have a cat hitting water. You had to have nerve to even contemplate entering the high dive enclosure. Most of us that did were trained swimmers but it didn't weaken the fright you felt while standing on the edge of the high dive board, looking down at that water that seemed miles below you. That first leap off was usually a heart stopping affair that was done close-eyed and with no attempt at a dive but more of a plain jump into the water. What was remarkable about the pool was that it didn't make a difference what you did from the board, whether it was a dive, a cannon ball, or just a jump into the water below; you always seemed to have enough momentum to carry to the bottom of the pool where you would kiss the concrete with your toes before swimming upwards to the surface again. That swim back to the surface was something because it felt as if the water was so deep that it took forever to come back up, even the sunlight down there was diffused and eerie-looking. After re-emerging, though, and swimming to the side to come out you had to feel as if you had finally accomplished something in your little life. You had your medal at last, you had jumped and survived, you had gone in a mouse and come out a man; chest all swollen up like a gorilla and you felt like thumping on it too but you didn't, you just went about your business as a kid but with the inner satisfaction of 'having done it' and knowing it.

For some reason the pools at the Beach closed long before the actual amusement park itself closed. Some people said it had to do with the eventual end of "the old south" segregation laws and the integration of the beach to all peoples of color and creed. To us kids all it meant was that another 'playground' of our youth had bitten the dust and gone under. It was no coincidence that even when the water had been drained from the pools and the gates padlocked up you still had kids faces pressed to the space in between the bars looking out over that cement expanse of emptiness and seeing the phantoms, the ghosts of the past and the expressions on their faces were such that they seemed to be hearing the splashing and squeals of delight of the shadows that were once there. For those of us that had passed the test of the high dive enclosure we hoped that maybe one day Mr. Batt would relent and re-open the pools, even just for a day, so we could feel that fear and excitement of going off the high dive just one more time. But for those kids that hadn't yet earned their badge it was a real tragedy. They must have felt that a real chance in life to be somebody had been taken away from them, that they had been robbed and now would not have the opportunity at redemption. To them, I say, forget it. There are plenty of 'high dive' tests in this life and if you didn't pass this one it's no big deal. No regrets, no regrets. However, the real tragedy of this situation is that the Beach itself is gone and that our children will never know what we knew as kids- the joy and fun of that entertainment, that playground that exists only in the mists of our memories now.

    For a while the Beach had a live stage area that was near the pools and built on the sands. The stage was a smallish white building that somehow resembled the cabin of a boat. It had a large platform for a roof that was the stage area. It was here on the sands of Lake Pontchartrain that the King of Rock-and-Roll, Elvis Presley, came and played on his way to super- stardom. The date was August 9th, 1956, and I'm sure that probably a million people would say they saw him there but the actual figure might be closer to a thousand. Still, a little white lie never hurt anybody and they were easy enough to work out in the confessional. The Batt brothers had the foresight to bring in talent that appealed to the teens and pre-teens of that era. He booked acts that were up-and-coming and that did not always mean musicians or singers; there were circus acts as well, magicians, acrobats, trapeze artists and people being shot out of giants canons into large nets. That was one of our favorites. The percussion of that canon being fired could be felt almost anywhere along the mid-way and the way that young woman or man was hurtled through the air into the net was an eternal mystery to us; how it was they were blown to bits by that explosion baffled us. The live acts on the sands at the Beach were usually held on Saturday nights and were an added attraction for the Beach's POP days and nights. POP Days were the immensely popular Pay-One-Price days when you didn't have to worry about fees for individual rides. You paid your fee and got your hand stamped and away you went to your favorite rides to ride until you either couldn't take it anymore or you threw-up, one or the other. We didn't understand how they could make any money with this kind of thing but what we failed to realize and we should have was that because of the length of lines one had to endure to get on that favorite ride was exactly what the Batts wanted to see.

They pulled in triple or quad attendance on those days and nights and were making a killing on concessions and games.

The mid-way games were the usual carnival variety, the air gun target-shoot, the bean-bag toss, the dart-throw and the famous milk bottle knock-down. For we guys, the milk bottle game was another one of those imaginary badges to shoot for from the Beach. Plenty of us didn't make it, for some reason or another when we stood up there behind the counter with those baseballs in our hands and looked at that pyramid of lead bottles with the crowd behind us our knees went limp and our aim disappeared. It seemed we could hit anything but those bottles but one had to admire the attendant, he was always standing too close to where that errant throw might go and get hit on the knee or the chest. A lot of the time we had the velocity but always just missed by a hair or two. Such is life. The Beach had its penny arcade and also a Skee-Ball building that had a unique looking sign out front of a flashing target with the word "Skee" vertically imposed below it. It was a real fixture on the mid-way. The building itself must have contained forty or fifty machines and the sounds of winning scores were always chirping about the room. People really loved to play Skee Ball back then so the room was crowded most of the time and it was a fact of Beach life that one had to wait a considerable amount of time to throw those wooden balls down the well-worn alleys. This was also one of those strange buildings to enter when it was empty like during mid-day before the evening rush of bowlers arrived. There always seemed to be too much air, too much space and very little noise. It was eerie to be there then.

The building that housed the penny arcade was located on the west side of the mid-way, very close to the Haunted House and very near the gigantic clown's head that became a lasting symbol of the Beach and its history. The arcade was every boy and girls dream world. It had coin operated games of every type and description. There were numerous pin-ball machines, miniature bowling machines, baseball, football and basketball games, there were target games with air-rifles and BBs and also the crane games that never grabbed the stuffed animals they were aimed at. The pinball machines were the most popular and most plentiful. Pinball games were a nickel so you'd put in a quarter and watch as five credits clicked over on the back glass. When you pressed the game button on the front of the machine you'd hear that magical sound of everything mechanical falling into place to begin the game and you could hear the balls dropping down from someplace deep inside the case. Most of us fancied ourselves pin-ball wizards back then and were addicts to the noise and sheer excitement of beating the game and hearing the free games click over. We'd skillfully put our hands on either corner of the box and assume our stance, we tapped on the flipper buttons to obtain our rhythm and we'd give the machine a little shove to make sure there was some give in its legs. That little shove was always a risk because the last thing one wanted to do was TILT the machine before ball number one ever got shot. It was a death-move to see that dreaded word appear on the glass; the lights went off and the flipper buttons perished while you watched as the ball in play fell harmlessly to the front of the machine and down out of view. More than anything it was a sign of 'NOT having the 'touch', a sure sign that one couldn't control themselves or the machine. TILT was a misery. The arcade was a place where you could either spend fifth teen minutes or two hours depending on one's skill with the games or, of course, how much change one had in ones pockets.

  The main attraction, however, of the mid-way were the rides and the Beach had a wide variety of them. There was the roller coaster, the Zephyr, with its red beacon atop the first hill that everyone looked for when approaching the vast parking lot of the grounds. The Wild Maus with its sharp turns and small chains that kept the cars grounded to the track. On the west side was the Haunted House, the Ferris wheel and the carousel which was housed in its own building with floor-to-ceiling mirrors for walls. Also on that end were the famous bumping cars that we spent hours at. We were practicing for our future lives driving the streets of New Orleans, trying desperately to avoid "this idiot and that idiot" as our father had termed most of the drivers in Gentilly. One had to envision potholes on the metallic floor, though, if you were truly to get the feel of New Orleans and its streets. Also on that end was a ride called the Paratrooper where you sat in a basket that resembled a giant mushroom which was connected along with ten or twelve other mushrooms to the hub of the mechanism by a large stem coming out of the top of the cap. They were all joined to the main hub by a large pin that allowed the ride to pivot as it spun around and began tilting upwards at an acute angle. At its apex the rider felt as if they would be thrown from the basket. On the east side of the mid-way was the Caterpillar which was a track ride that traveled up and down. The cars were circular and big enough to get ten or twelve people shoulder-to-shoulder in one. It wasn't unusual to be shoved into someone's chest that you didn't know as the cars picked up speed. Next to the Caterpillar were the infamous Flying Scooters. They were sort of a sailboat of the sky and very popular with the patrons. The compartment had a large vertical wing in front that resembled the main sail of a boat. You could move this sail left or right by hand as the ride spun around. The scooter was connected to the hub by a long metal chain that allowed for the car to go almost horizontal as the velocity increased. It wasn't so much a scary ride as it was a ride that one felt you had some measure of control over. With careful manipulation of the sail you could take the car on a higher to lower path. We were always trying to be as reckless as we could with our manipulations of the sail. For some inexplicable reason we thought an erratic path was the best one; the rebellion of youth again. The Flying Scooters was the only ride I remember hearing and reading about that a near tragic accident occurred. It seemed one night that one of the cars chains broke and sent a group of riders into the crown of an oak tree nearby. As kids we longed for such notoriety. Also on the east end was a ride whose name escapes me but could have been called Rotor or Rooter (not the plumbing kind). This was a large cylinder that you entered which had stand-up compartments all along it's circumference. There were also handrails on either side that you'd hold onto as this ride spun around at a growing rate. As it did so the wheel that you were part of titled upwards and you were almost vertical at the apex. It was one of those rides where centrifugal force pinned you against the wall and no matter how hard you tried you just couldn't peel yourself away from it. This was one of those times when you walked very un-steadily off the gangplank when the ride was over. It was also a ride to stay off of if you had just eaten dinner.

  The Beach was definitely a family place, especially families with small children. On the west side of the mid-way was Kiddie Land with junior versions of some of the Beaches most popular rides. It was always filled with moms and dads and their young ones. The squeals of delight emanating from that section were always loud and plentiful. In the Kiddie Land section of the park stood a white light house that also became an icon of the park. Years later we learned of its historic significance when many of us presumed it had been built for the Beach like the clowns head we learned that it was a hundred years old and marked a community and resort area of New Orleans called Milneburg. It was the first resort area that New Orleanians had come to as far back as the 1830's and it had disappeared, probably as a result of Prohibition during the Jazz Age, right beneath the sands of the Beach.   There were also covered picnic areas scattered throughout the park where you could come with a large group of people and spend the entire day swimming, eating and playing. A day like that was a real treat for any of us growing up in Gentilly and New Orleans. What punctuated those nights for us Gentillians that lived near the park were the fireworks shows that were put on for certain holidays of the year. Hordes of people went out to the Lakefront on those nights to await the pyrotechnics. For those of us that lived close by we could walk out of our doors at nine o'clock, lean up against the hood of our parent's cars, talk about the day with our friends and watch the black sky until it was lit up by Technicolor streamers and sparks. As kids we always felt privileged to live so close. For us it was within walking distance of our homes. We knew that when the doors closed for good in 1983 that something large and meaningful had passed from our lives. We lamented that our children and their children would not have a chance to make Beach memories. We supposed that Harry couldn't keep it going for whatever reason but it did bring tears to our eyes to see it shut down but we didn't blame him for it; instead we silently thanked him for his vision, for his dream brought so much fun and joy into our lives. Wherever you are, Harry, you made a few generations of New Orleanians a lot richer with happiness.

  And now for a few personal notes. First, to my two older sisters who begged me for the singer, Leslie Gore's autograph. I must plead innocence by way of ignorance and stupidity. Although I must admit that my athletic ability enabled me to predict the flight of that piece of cardboard that it was scribbled on so well as to be able to snatch it from the air (I actually saw it fall harmlessly to the ground beyond the outstretched arms of twenty or thirty screaming teenagers gathered behind the stage of the Beach's sands). I know that I put in in the bag with my army soldiers and their tanks. Is it my fault that it somehow got lost during a battle along the way? Also apologies need to be issued to the two girls that the Big Lou and I followed the whole night (felt more like two years) up-and-down the mid-way. Whenever I worked up the courage to go and talk to them the Big Lou would chicken out and vice versa. It was such a comedy of errors and mistiming that we felt as if we missed the opportunity at the loves of our lives or at least for the summer. You know, Lou, it felt like we did that same thing an awful lot on those hot, summer nights. Still, you were great company and I don't regret a minute spending time with your ugly self and the dream of having a girl like Annette on my arm was still alive and kicking. Actually, I'd do it all over again and I did with you….. many, many times.

CHAPTER IX
'YATS CAN THROW TOO

For us young kids growing up in Gentilly Mardi Gras was strictly a family affair. It was a fantastic time of year with personal memories that were no different from the kids down the street. When we got home we'd compare catches and maybe make some trades on too-many of one kind of parade doubloons or trinkets. What we noticed about fat Tuesday and the few weeks leading up to it was that it seemed more borne out of Catholicism which was the predominant religion of the late 50's and early 60's than anything else and this was a strange dichotomy for us to digest as kids. What did Holy Religion have to do with a festival that seemed hedonistic, almost pagan in its origins? We found it hard to understand how our church could be interlaced with a festival that at any other time of year would be considered taboo by the nuns who taught us and the priests who sermonized us. We hadn't a clue why on a certain Tuesday in February or March it was okay to laugh and play all day with a costume and mask on when we felt as if we should be in school. Of course it was alright with us but we didn't understand why. What really confused us was why it was permitted on that certain Tuesday and then strictly forbidden on the Wednesday immediately after it. We knew that on the next day we would go to church and have a tiny dot of ash thumbed on our foreheads by the priest. We also knew we would not be eating meat on Fridays for a very long time. It was indeed a strange time of year for us kids, a time of year fueled with contradictions and immense joy.

Mardi Gras back then was mostly a native affair. It seemed strictly designed and held for our enjoyment and not for the California or New York tourists. Celebrities often came to the Crescent City to see the festivities but back then they rarely if at all partook of floatriding and related festivities; never mind about being asked to be a king or queen of a krewe. As kids we weren't aware of the influx of tourists during Mardi Gras. We knew they were there but mostly confined to the narrow streets of the French Quarter or to the bleachers near St. Charles and Canal and they always seemed to be surrounded by armed policemen. Back then we believed that this was not so much for their protection as it was for ours. Our police were making sure that the foreigners would not escape and somehow ruin our fun with their strange ideas and ways.

As a young Catholic School kid Mardi Gras was the only time of year that one stepped outside of one's Parish and commingled with children from other parts of the city. Most of the other areas of town were as foreign to us as Egypt is to Texas. We might find ourselves playing with a group of kids from Edward the Confessor Parish and we usually went, "huh, where?" For most of us Orleanians our earliest memory of Mardi Gras is almost always a photograph of us with a sibling sitting in the box atop a ladder with our fathers behind us. There are probably hundreds of thousands of pictures like that floating around in photo albums all over Orleans Parish and each one of them is special and priceless to its owner.

Because Mardi Gras is such a personal factory of memories I must relate mine as a major part of this chapter. As a youngster we rode in one of the two truck parades that followed Rex on Fat Tuesday; Elks Orleanians. Our Parish, St. Raphael the Arch Angel, built a theme-set on top of a flatbed trailer that Mack Trucks pulled. It took quite an effort to get the truck ready for the big day with the men of the parish devoting most of their evenings and weekends to building it and painting while the women used their skills of sewing and to make the costumes that all the participants would wear from adults to the littlest child. Everyone that rode was costumed with that year's theme. One time it was the nursery rhyme, The Old Lady In The Shoe, so we were all dressed as waifs and small children with yellow wigs on and big red striped socks. The following year the theme was taken from the Jerry Lee Lewis song, 'Great Balls of Fire" and we had on costumes of yellow, orange and red sequins with hats that consisted of styrofoam balls that were sequined in the same color scheme and had colored foil shooting from the hats in rays. The women really spent a lot of time on those costumes and it reflected with the truck winning one of the Best in Show Awards for that year. The truck parades, Elks and Crescent City, were specifically designed to get folks involved with Mardi Gras that otherwise couldn't afford to get involved. It was a way for the middle class to experience what it was like to ride the float and be on the throwing end of the beads and trinkets. For us kids it was a matter of great importance that we had tons of throws to pitch out especially considering we could exercise little control as to the quantity that we threw out and when. What this jargon means is that most of us threw our stuff way before the truck even rolled in the parade. It was an early morning that everyone boarded the decorated flatbed, maybe four or five in the AM while all the preparations for the actual ride were still being made. Then as the float was being hauled to the staging area we threw to anyone that was standing around. That could be other kids from other floats or people that lived around the streets where the staging areas were. When our throws were gone we often went into our parents or siblings throw bags and began pilfering their stuff. It was an angry parent that finally settled into their positions when the parade began who reached into their bag to throw out some beads or trinkets and found the bag nearly empty. If you weren't lucky you could get lit into right then and there on the float. After a few years of this you finally learned a lesson and waited to pilfer the stuff at the right moments; namely near the middle of the ride when the parents had had one too many drinks. Float riding came with its own experience.

When the trucks began to roll it was a fantastic sight for we kids to witness. Spectators were everywhere. It was a sea of ladders and small children sitting atop them with their parents arms around them. It was whole families decked out in costumes themselves picnicking on the neutral grounds and throwing their hands up while eating cold fried chicken and cold slaw. It was young girls giggling and imploring that you throw them something, anything. The 'throw me something' chant was pervasive, inescapable. Even when you were out of throws and could do nothing but shrug your shoulders at them, it still came, and they still pleaded for something. It was at this stage of the ride that we would be tearing pieces of the float off and throwing that to the pleading masses of humanity that were below us and moving by fast. Many a parishioner that didn't ride that year wanted to know why the float looked so torn up and barren at the end of the ride. It was the wind, we'd tell them, and the wind was blowing up a storm and tearing the float up. Sure, they'd say, sure.

What people fail to realize today is that we were the pioneers back then. It was through our ingenuity and experience that the riders of today have such an easy time of it. Case in point; one year the men of the parish designed and built a beautiful float that encompassed an infrastructure that was broad as it was tall. It was a massive sight to see, beautifully decorated with colored foils and crepes. We were attracting plenty of attention while rolling to the staging area. Plenty of heads were being turned by this sure winner of ours. We just knew that this was the year we'd ride off with that huge golden 'Best Designed Truck' of the year trophy. However, our brilliant designers neglected to take into account the height and breath of some of our famous underpasses throughout the city. We were turning heads alright, none more so than the heads that turned our way when we got wedged underneath one of the underpasses on N. Broad or Gentilly Blvd. Those turned heads had smiles and smirks aplenty when power saws had to be brought out to cut some of the floats height away in order for us to pass underneath it. Did we worry about it? Heck no, we continued on like nothing had happened and had a good time of it and there was always next year for the trophy but from then on float builders had to take into account the height limit of the city's underpasses to prevent a similar occurrence.

    During the era of the 1950's and early 1960's Mardi Gras parades were strictly confined to the Uptown Downtown to French Quarter routes. In the late 60's parades began to fan out all over not only Orleans Parish but also Jefferson and St. Bernard Parishes. The two in Gentilly that drew krewe members from all over the local area were Hercules and Pandora. They began their run in the late 60's and were both night parades that took what became the traditional Gentilly route; they lined up in the Pontchartrain Beach parking lot and rolled through the traffic round-about and in front of the iconic entrance to the Beach down the west side of Elysian past Ferrara's on Robert E. Lee. Onward they'd go past St. Raphael Church and school; the heart of the Parish. At Mirabeau they all took the turn to the west towards Paris Avenue crossing over St. Anthony Street and past Pap's Supermarket and the McKenzie's stand-alone store at the corner of the parking lot. Once past Pap's the parades would cross over the London Avenue Canal by way of the Mirabeau Bridge. At Paris they turned south back towards the lake and into the heart of Parkchester Estates past Cabrini church and school, the other parish that both krewes drew heavily from. At Robert E. Lee Blvd. they turned eastward, just catching the corner of the upper middle class neighborhood of Lake Terrace and Jean Gordon School built close to the levees of the London Avenue Canal. Here they crossed over the canal for the second time; this also took them past Ferrara's for the second time; the only business that the parades passed twice on their routes. At Elysian Fields again they would turn south past the iconic Pitt Theater for the short ride back to the Beach parking lot. Sadly, by 1983 they vanished from the streets of Gentilly, much to our dismay but for those years they gave the adults and kids of the area their own piece of Mardi Gras and we didn't have to go downtown or to the Quarter to see them; we'd just hop over the back yard fence through our neighbors yard and onto Elysian where we'd look for our friends and relatives who had reserved spots along the street or neutral ground with their ladders out in front of their parked pickup trucks. For a while everybody was there and it was one vast party, our own party that led up to the traditional Fat Tuesday celebrations.

Unfortunately, the Gentilly parades didn't have the staying power of a Rex or Endymion and disappeared from the Mardi Gras calendar, it seemed, all too soon. Was there something jaded in having too many Mardi Gras Parades? Mardi Gras has a way of weeding out the also-rans. Go down to Mardi Gras Fountain on the Lakefront and read all the plaques surrounding it and you will see just how many parades and krewes have gone out of existence. The mainstay krewes are there through thick and thin, the others are relegated to the memories of individuals like me. They were fun while they lasted but we knew they would come to an end. Somehow we knew that the sight of floats and bands moving past the Pitt and Lawrence's Bakery was something we'd never see again; just as we knew the matinees or the glazed would disappear and would never come again. Those were the golden years of our youth, when you think, believe that life will not change, that things will stay the same forever until one day you wake up and realize that they've already gone; but you thank God for it anyway because at least we had the privilege of experiencing it even if it was for too short of a time.

Now to relate a personal memory. I'm sure if she knew my name the woman who was standing way back near the column at Lee Circle on St. Charles, would thank me for throwing her the one pair of beads I had left. They were a pair of beautiful glass beads probably made in Czechoslovakia like so many were before the influx of Japanese and Chinese throws. It was a great throw for a southpaw and because I'm such a humble guy I feel it should be related frame-by-frame. Like most Gentillians I am a huge fan of the underdog. I prayed every year for Tulane to upset LSU in the annual rivalry game (cried and was there when it finally happened for the first time in thirty something years). I prayed every year that the Saints would win the Super Bowl, we were the champions of the underprivileged and deserving masses who for whatever reason always, always found themselves on the short end of the stick. So it was on this particular Mardi Gras with only one pair of beads left to my name to throw and because my sisters were jealously hoarding theirs that I spotted a lovely, yet forlorn looking girl; gorgeous and beautiful standing at the base of Lee's column while rounding the circle. She was forlorn looking because standing where she was with her boyfriend she had precisely zero beads draped around her neck. They were miles from the front rows and certainly out of reach of most throws; that is, most mortal throwers. As we slowly rounded the circle with my lone pair of beads being twirled on the index finger of my right hand I spotted her or rather, I should say, we spotted each other. It was one of those enchanted moments. She perked up immediately when she saw that she had my attention. She put both her arms high in the air and implored me to make an attempt at the throw. It seemed others had tried and probably failed by many miserable feet before. The possibility of failure did not enter my mind as I stood bolt upright at the trucks rail and in one fluid motion transferred the beads from my right hand into the palm of my left. As I did so, the beads seemed to ball themselves perfectly so as to make an ideal weight in which to be tossed. It was one of those times when the tumblers click into place and the universal lock mysteriously but inevitably opens. I reached way back with my left arm, just lightly shoving myself away from the rail with my right hand and arm, transferring all my weight to my left leg, winding myself up for the throw. My right foot and leg left the floor of the truck just as a pitchers leaves the mound and as I began the move forward my right leg planted itself firmly on the floor again. My left arm swung high and released the missile just past the apex of the arc that was created. In other words, velocity, baby, speed was created by an eleven year old that otherwise should not be capable of it. The beads sailed over the outstretched arms and fingers of what seemed like hundreds on its way to the target. At first they climbed a bit the way an arced throw usually does but as they began to descend some of the outstretched fingers on some of those outstretched arms seemed very close to snatching them in mid-flight. I believe there was not more than an inch or two gap between that last arm and finger at the lowest point of the throw. As it landed perfectly in the hands of that beautiful girl a hush came over the crowd as it mulled over what just had occurred. They all knew that what they had seen was rarely possible but it was Mardi Gras when such rarities can become the norm. As the truck rolled onwards, natural time and motion seemed to resume. The girl, though, surprised herself that the beads had made it, quickly waved them with one hand and blew me a kiss with the other. We continued to laugh and the crowd continued to scream for more. I was empty handed but satisfied and knew it was a moment to remember.

CHAPTER X
"HE HAS RED HAIR!"

Every new invention eventually finds its way down the socio-economic ladder especially after mass production kicks in. During the late fifties and early sixties most of us remember television in strictly black-and-white images; or more aptly, beige and gray. Now, this is meant literally as well as figuratively because most of our parents couldn't afford the latest advance in media technology: color television. All our favorite television shows were shaded in mono-tones. We couldn't tell what color the dress Mary Tyler Moore was wearing on the Dick Van Dyke Show or if the khaki's Ernest Borgnine had on during McHale's Navy were really the color of khaki. Of course you never wondered about such things if all you saw were varying shades of beige and gray. It's when you see the other side that your mind begins to wonder. For us that happened at our grandparents' house who were not so much rich as one could say just well-off. They bought a console color television before any of us kids knew that color television even existed. For a while we would go over there every Sunday and watch Tinkerbell paint the Disney logo in bright pastel colors or we'd see just how green the grass was on the Cartwright ranch in the latest TV western, Bonanza. Watching color TV after years of seeing just beige and gray was a dream, like some un-reality that we knew wasn't the norm. We thought at first that the color we saw wasn't real but manufactured for us in some strange way. This wasn't our world and the real world, our world, was never bathed in such vibrant color. In those days we very rarely saw celebrities. As kids we watched the shows that made us laugh, not the ones that brought sadness or tears. For us that meant that the news programs were as foreign to our minds as someplace named, Yugoslavia. Besides, most of us were in bed way before the news made its nightly ten PM appearance. Somehow, though, we sensed that what our parents were seeing and listening to on those broadcasts was vastly different than the sensationalist, violence ridden newscasts of today.

Of course, the older one got the more aware one became of the world around them. My sister and I were still in elementary school when our mother decided to give us a day off and take us somewhere where we would see the President of the United States. It was early May of 1962 and although we were young we had become aware that our President was a very young man and that he was married to a young woman and had kids that were just a little younger than us. At that time we did not understand the significance of such a thing; however, I do recall that my mother said that her father took her somewhere when she was a girl to see Franklin Delano Roosevelt before the advent of WWII. However, if all we had to do to get a day off of school was to go and see the President of the United States when he comes to town we secretly hoped he would come our way more often; say once or twice a month at least. It was not a hot day, in fact, a rare May cold front had come through and the air was crisp that morning, chilly enough for our mom to put sweaters on us. I seem to remember her being in a blue sweater and scarf when she loaded us into the car and took off down Carrolton Avenue past City Park to Palmyra Street where we stood on the banks of a recently cemented lined canal. It was a beautiful day, no clouds and bright sun-shine. Mom had her trademark dark sunglasses on. My sister and I squinted into the sunlight. When you're that age you usually have no idea from what direction the cavalcade will be coming so most of the time you are looking in both directions at once to make sure you don't miss anything when it finally arrives. We were probably looking in the opposite direction because before we realized it some black limousines began moving past us at a fast pace. As we turned to see them I recognized our mayor of New Orleans riding in an open top limo. Right after him another limo came by with the President himself waving to the people lining both sides of the street. I turned to mom in amazement and screamed, "momma, look, he has red hair like you"! After a few years of seeing him in mono-tones it was a realization to see someone like that in every day color. Mom and he had almost the exact same hair color. Maybe that was why she brought us to see him. Maybe she felt close to him. It was a day I would never forget. Unfortunately, as far as JFK was concerned there would be a few more days that most of us would like to forget but never will. For this moment, though, it was a happy contented sort of day. We felt close to the man who was the youngest ever elected President and one of the few that was Catholic. That brought him into focus for us. Mom and dad were young too, we were Catholic and 'Shazaam', he had red hair like mom!

  Less than 18 months later, while sitting in Sister Beatrice's fifth grade classroom in the late morning the principal of the school, Sister Bernadine, made an announcement over the loud-speaker. It was a historic announcement for every one of us and it was a plea for prayer. The date was November 22, 1963. Sister Bernadine told us bluntly that John Fitzgerald Kennedy has been shot in Dallas, Texas and that all of us should say a prayer for his survival. An hour later the President of the United States was dead and our lives changed forever. We had been privy to a defining American moment. For the rest of our lives we would remember where we were on that fateful day when we got the news, but for our parents that meant two defining moments. They treated December 7th, 1941 the same way. The day the Japanese bombed Pearl Harbor and ushered America into World War II my father was working in a gas station, my mother was in class. They never forgot that day either. For me, I could not forget the image of the smiling, very much alive man with red hair like my mom who I saw just the previous year. For most of us young kids who had not really experienced a death of any type yet it was a strange, solemn period and the next four days was a microcosm of death and grief that touched all American lives. As children we grew up a bit after witnessing the shock and disbelief that someone so important could be gunned down in such a public place during such a public moment; we were just as numb while watching the almost perverted transfer of power from JFK to LBJ later that evening and the hasty removal of the dead from Dallas with his wife's dress still smudged with her husband's blood, we were sick to our stomachs and had no appetite after seeing the coffin leave the plane and be loaded into a non-descript Navy ambulance for the trip to the White House, everything, including time seemed to be suspended in slow motion and the fact that it was day or night seemed to make no difference to us, we were all glued to the television sets in our living rooms, our regular programs, when shown, appeared lifeless and mundane in the face of such tragic events and the drama kept unfolding. The man suspected of the assassination had been arrested and taken to jail, we hungered to see him, we needed a face for our anger and rage to spill out upon, we sensed a need for revenge so someone stuck a gun in the suspects stomach and murdered him on live TV for all the nation to see; Lee Harvey Oswald was the first real televised murder, the censors could not stop the cameras from showing it to us, they could not stop reality from unfolding. So we continued the deathwatch, we were there while the flag draped coffin was removed to the same caisson that was used to carry Lincoln's body during another assassination and state funeral almost a century ago, and when John Kennedy Jr. made his famous salute in the child-like innocence and perfect maturity of a three year old on the steps of the Capitol we choked with emotion, the display of national grief was immense and almost too much to bear. For once we did not complain about our black-and-white TV sets because our emotions and our mood fit the color of what was broadcast and the grayness and chill that pervaded those November days in 1963 were appropriate, maybe too much so. Somehow we knew that Jacqueline Kennedy was not wearing her trademark pink on this day, we knew that her dress was black the same as we knew that his brothers were wearing black and gray suits. We sat and watched as the procession slowly wound its way through the streets of Washington D.C. with a conglomerate of world leaders and royalty slowly walking behind in solemn lockstep. We knew they were there but we were focused on the six matched horses pulling the caisson bearing the casket of our young Catholic President, we blankly stared at our sets and wondered if we were really in our living rooms or there in person because our feelings seemed so real. We wondered how his wife, now a widow, could be so brave. She must have been very frightened, she was right beside her husband when those bullets tore apart his body, surely she must have thought that she too was going to die. We wondered how it was that she was not falling down with grief during these sad three days following his death. Whenever the cameras trained on her she appeared unbowed with her head up, so brave in grief. Even as small children we sensed that this was a very special lady, our love and interest in her would never wane. When at graveside, after the flag that had draped the coffin was carefully folded and handed to her we at last saw some sign of her sorrow when she held her hand to her veil-covered mouth and choked back a sob. When we saw that we knew it was all right for us to do the same so we cried and choked on our emotions. I believe it was by her hand that the torch that is supposed to burn eternally by his grave was lit. It was as appropriate as that sob that the nation finally witnessed coming from so majestic a lady.

  Something extra had been lost with America losing its leader so violently, something as tangible as the funeral that followed. Some of her innocence and goodwill evaporated along with the smoke from that hot rifle barrel. From that day forward, in the eyes of the rest of the world, we became a violent, crime ridden society. As a nation we did nothing to stem that portrayal of us while Robert Kennedy lay on a kitchen floor in some LA hotel with a bullet to the brain or Martin Luther King lay dying on some hotel balcony in Memphis. We have done nothing but enhance the image. Public assassination came into vogue after we lost JFK, for a while it was 'open season' on politicians and celebrities. Maybe it is time we wake up from our slumber and do something about it. Being in the public eye may seem like a glamorous life to some but to others it must be a very frightening proposition. It is no mystery that most of the best and brightest would want to stay out of view of the general populace because it seems fame can bring violence with it. For those that are in the lens of the camera too often they must wonder if they are not in the sights of some gun toting lunatic somewhere. It's then when anonymity seems healthy.

CHAPTER XI
GENTILLY CUISINE

Messina's Sweet Shop- corner of Pressburg and Marigny.
Circa- 2006 after Katrina and prior to demolition.

Strange but one of the things I remember most about Gentilly food was the old knob-pull candy machine in the laundromat at the corner of Elysian Fields and Robert E. Lee.

It was the first time I had ever tasted a Zero candy bar and its sweet nougat core covered in white chocolate. It melted in your mouth and the taste of white chocolate seemed sweeter yet subtler to dark or milk chocolate. For children growing up in the 1950's and 1960's candy was an essential part of our worlds. Those close to St. Raphael School marveled at the color and collection of confections at Messina's Sweet Shop on the corner of Marigny and Pressburgs Street. Here they could obtain their favorite 10cent Hubigs Pies, lemon or apple was always one of mine; or you could get the candy straws with a sweet-tart confection colored in all the colors of the rainbow or the pleasant nougat of the paper covered Mary Janes, similar to the larger Bit-A-Honey bars which could suck the fillings out of your teeth. Jaw Breakers of every size and flavor could be had as well as Peppermint Sticks of green and red. Red Hots were also there and they would turn your tongue crimson with their hot cinnamon taste. Sno-Caps and Milk Duds were also we kids favorite small cardboard box candies. Of the candy bars the ever popular and age-old favorites were readily available; Snickers, Milky Ways, Butterfingers, Reese's Peanut Butter Cups, Heath Bars and foil covered Chunky bars which was the first time we had had raisins and chocolate combined, an interesting taste. Messina's might also have been the venue for a lot of kids having their first bag of Cheetos. Back then the bag was an opaque plastic all in yellow with a small window in front that showed the curly sticks of cheesy goodness. Potato chips were also to be had but only the salted variety was bagged; flavored potato chips didn't evolve until much later. Frito corn chips, though, were there and the bag has pretty much stayed exactly the same. Cracker Jacks was also on the shelf only back then the prizes were much better; just ask anyone and they will tell you. Of course, most of these items could be bought at any local grocery store or convenience store but for those kids living in the St. Raphael or McDonough 39 school areas Messina's was the place to go.

It's old screen door and small room has survived in kid's memories all these years.

Of the bakeries in Gentilly Lawrences, at the southwest corner of Elysian Fields and Filmore Avenues was probably the most popular. Lawrence Aiavolasiti studied baking in France and eventually returned to his birthplace, New Orleans, and opened his bakery in Gentilly. For years he had a picture of himself and a tiered wedding cake on the façade of the building. The story was that if you had 'Mr. Wedding Cake' bake your cake he would show up at the reception and slice it for you for free. But wedding cakes weren't his only specialty; his glaze and cream and jelly donuts filled the air with sweet aroma in the early mornings when the daily baking was just beginning. They did sliced cakes of almost every type and description and just about every person had their favorite but their doberge and red-velvet varieties were their most popular. You could also buy these in small square sizes or bon-bon size for two bits each or four for a dollar. Lawrence's red velvet cake still remains the stuff of Gentilly legend. The question gets asked several times a year if anyone knows someone or has the recipe to his confectionary gem but unfortunately he may have taken it to the grave with him when he passed away in 1999 at the age of 88. Hopefully he has a spot in heaven where those aromas can still be sensed. God is being well fed.

There were a few more bakeries that Gentillians knew. McKenzie's opened two branch stores; one on Elysian Fields across from Ferrara's supermarket and another on the corner of Mirabeau and St. Anthony. McKenzie's donuts were its forte; the cream, jelly and glaze were all very tasty but later they developed what they called its 'buttermilk drops' and a New Orleans tradition was born. After mass on Sundays plenty of families went here to get their dozen 'drops' and maybe some cinnamon rolls to take home and warm up to spread butter on. These were delicious eaten in that fashion.

However, McKenzie's, was known for another branch store that not only had confectionaries but also fried chicken. Their 'Chicken In A Box' store on the corner of Frenchman and Gentilly Blvd. produced a different aroma but one equally craved by many a Gentillian.

On Verbena Street a few blocks off Franklin Avenue was another Gentilly bakery that generally had no signs or fancy advertising. It was housed in the rear of either a garage or the ground level of a two-story home. Verbena's produced hot donuts almost on demand and bagged them in the brown paper lunch bags of school days. Most people ate them before they got home because the smell was too irresistible to deny. Eating half a dozen on the fly was easy to do and plenty had to go back for more.

The restaurants of Gentilly in the mid-50's and 1960's were not that many but what was there was quality food. As a child our family outing I believe took place on a weekday night when we all piled into the car and went to eat at the A & G Cafeteria on Gentilly Blvd. It was in a strip mall on the northwest corner of Elysian Fields and Gentilly on the lower floor with a Western Auto Store on the one corner. Above it was the well-known women's store, Gus Mayer. The fashionable women of Gentilly all shopped there. The A &G was renowned for its stuffed eggplant dish that was served in a small bowl with a dusting of fine breadcrumbs on top. The entrees were mostly varied, there was baked fish, sliced roast beef, Salisbury steak with mashed potatoes and brown gravy and its very popular fried chicken. It was here that I first tasted a wedge of iceberg lettuce covered in Roquefort dressing. My mother used to get it every time we went and she always saved some for me. It was a taste not for everyone but to this day it is still one of my favorites. For desert their cherry pie and vanilla ice cream was the best capper to the meal and for we kids there was always a colored balloon in the lattice work near the cashiers' station. We just had to go home with a balloon on a stick.

On Friday nights our father would go to Teddy's Grill on Franklin Avenue and bring home either a whole loaf of Roast Beef on French or a sack full of hamburgers; or sometimes both. Our first experience with a po-boy was from Teddy's but it certainly wasn't our last. Occasionally, the family would be taken out to Chef Hwy. and a restaurant called, Martin Brothers. It was here that I tasted my first oyster po-boy. It was a delectable blend of lightly toasted French bread, shredded lettuce and sliced tomatoes slathered in tartar sauce with about a dozen perfectly fried oysters sandwiched in between. On the plate were golden French fries accompanying the sandwich. We struggled to eat it all but we looked forward with great anticipation to our next visit so we could try and do it all over again. It would be a few years before oysters on the half-shell were introduced to us. The eating of raw seafood was going to take some time getting used to; although as a child I remember going fishing and sneaking a taste or two of the raw shrimp we were using for bait. Sushi hadn't been imported into American cuisine back then. We weren't quite ready for it yet.

Geographically speaking, the east side of Gentilly ended for us at the Peoples Avenue Canal but then Gentilly Woods shopping center and subdivision was developed and Gentilly expanded to the Industrial Canal and a bit beyond it. Besides Martin Brothers the best seafood around was near Lakefront Airport on Haynes Blvd. Haynes ran from Downman Road all the way out to Little Woods. There were many camps across the street where New Orleans families spent weekends or entire summers on the waters of Lake Pontchartrain so they could enjoy the cool summer lake breezes. The restaurants across the street tapped into the abundance of seafood in the lake. The Lakeview Restaurant was one of them and a unique New Orleans entrée was born; the Seafood Boat. The

Lakeview seemed to be one of those neighborhood restaurants that started off in a smallish building and then began expanding piecemeal it seemed with thin plywood walls and floors that had soft spots in them. It was rare to go there and find tables open and the wait for food seemed inordinately long but then the orders were prepared on demand and frying all that seafood up always took time. The wait was worth it, especially for the 'Boat'. It was a high loaf of white bread, of which the top was cut off and the inside scooped out. Butter and garlic was then brushed into the hollowed out inside and also on the underneath side of the top. Into the middle fried oysters were piled in and the lid put back on. French fries were put around the boat and the whole thing taken out to the table. It was an imposing sight sitting there and the aroma caused the salivary glands to kick in. One could also get the half-and-half which came with half oysters and half shrimp. Even the bread proved too delectable to leave behind. The combination of melted butter and fried seafood lying inside gave the bread an irresistible taste. Sadly, the Lakeview closed in the mid 1980's but its signature dish can still be found at some seafood restaurants in Jefferson or Orleans. Now if we could only get the cost down to where it was back then we'd really be doing good.

  Another restaurant on Haynes that is fondly remembered was Gee and Lills. It was only a few blocks from the Lakeview and offered the traditional seafood fare. There were delectable seafood plates as well as the gigantic seafood platters. One could spoon gumbo down or eat raw oysters dipped into horseradish and ketchup and put whole on Saltines. If memory serves, Gee and Lills used to have a dinner plate night that would include some Italian food. Of the fish that was eaten and those days, Speckled Trout and Red Snapper seemed to be the favorites. The popular entrée, Trout Amandine, was almost always Speckled Trout. Most of the fish dishes back then were usually baked or broiled or lightly pan fried. Strange to say, but as a child I don't recall eating catfish. The saltwater catfish or 'hard heads' as they were known were too bloody and too hard to skin. They were basically a 'trash fish' but also one to be weary of especially in the boat as their sharp fins could puncture your skin and deliver a painful toxin into your bloodstream that would sting for hours. Also, I don't recall eating all that much crawfish in the 50's and 60's and I don't believe they were listed on the menus. The crawfish boils of today weren't in existence back then. We had to wait for Al Scramuzza and Seafood City to bring them to the populace. But boiled crabs and shrimp were always in abundance and the blue crabs of Lake Pontchartrain are renowned for their orange fat back then as they still are today. Crabs were usually eaten with Saltines and cocktail sauce; shrimp the same way. Tartar sauce was sometimes served but it was usually a pinkish blend of mayo and ketchup with minced dill, not mostly mayo as it is today.

  Breakfast fare in Gentilly was a little harder to find than lunch and dinner. Of the ones that I remember, Richards, the unique little triangular building that sat in the triangular lot at Old Gentilly Road and Chef Hwy was one of the favorites. They were open 24 hours and so they served all three meal times. Their eggs over easy with grits and bacon and biscuits was the breakfast staple. Also, a local restaurant named Joe Joes operated for a while on Elysian Fields between Robert E. Lee and New Mexico Street. Joe Joes became locally famous for their chicken liver omelets usually cooked up on Sunday mornings after Catholic services at St. Raphael. For a while there was a small diner that existed underneath the high billboard signs at the southwest corner of Elysian Fields and Gentilly Blvd. They weren't there very long but their biscuits were quite good. If Gentillians weren't dining out for breakfast they seemed to be quite satisfied with taking home cinnamon rolls from Lawrence's or McKenzie's and spreading butter on them after warming them up a touch in their ovens.

Of course buttermilk drops, glazed donuts and coffee cakes were also very tasty out of the oven.

Every Gentillian had their favorites. Some of those that deserves mention are as follows: Whiteys on Downman Road that doubled as a pool hall and seafood restaurant, Morrison's Cafeteria on Chef Hwy. in the Gentilly Shopping Center (their Shrimp Plate was quite good), Sclafani's on Haynes Blvd, an old world tablecloth restaurant that served Italian food, the Howard Johnson's on Old Gentilly Road that served a plethora of pancakes, Slicky's on Prentiss Avenue next to the old Golden Que pool hall, Luigi's on Elysian Fields close to New Mexico Street served the best pizza in Gentilly, Vazquez's on Franklin Avenue and Filmore also served lunch and dinner, the Bakery across the street next to Teddy's Grill was always crowded at lunch with people wanting their Po-Boys, the Steer Inn on Elysian Fields close to Robert E. Lee became the classic drive-in for burgers and malts in Gentilly. Most, if not all, are now gone but the memory of their food lives on.

CHAPTER XII
GENTILLY INSPIRED FICTION & POETRY

THE SEAWALL

Pellinore, the family dog chases waves on the bottom steps of the Lake Pontchartrain sea-wall.

They met every day on the seawall. It was always before sunrise so they just extended silent greetings. Then they sat down together on the top step and lit up cigarettes. While unrolling their crab nets they would talk. Yes, they would talk, and as they spoke they saw their conversation ushering in the dawn, changing the lamp black into a slowly brightening violet.

First they talked about the past and some regrets over poor decisions made years ago. They encapsulated the past and moved on to the present. Then they spoke of children, grandchildren and lovingly about their wives. World affairs had a turn and here the differences between them became pronounced. One was a liberal with the thoughts that freedom should be afforded to people everywhere and that included this country where all people are or should be created equal regardless of color, creed or gender. The other was a strict conservative tending towards the isolationist view; coming to the conclusion that Americans should let the rest of the world stew in their own pots. The Middle East was the hot topic of the day especially since the liberal had a tinge of Jewish blood in him. This was well used by the conservative, he always cutting conversations short with, "well, you're just Jewish, that's all".

To the liberal it all boiled down to a pessimist and an optimist; to the other it was simply a matter of a realist trying to impress reality on a romantic idealist. Although they rarely agreed in certain areas of conversation they both came away with a strange respect for the others opinion.

The sun was rising by the time they got world affairs out of the way so they walked with nets in hand down the seawall. Soon, the surface of the calm lake was shattered with the throwing out of the nets. They threw out eight each with the bait firmly tied into them and spaced some ten yards apart. When all the lines were secured they'd go back to the top step and light up another cigarette. Their wooden hampers sat together a few feet in back of them in the shade of a young oak and for the people that happened by on their way to work the sight must had seemed somewhat odd. The two men never took notice of what was going on behind them in the street. They just smoked and talked with their eyes always out over the water.

The two would continue with their morning conversation, talking of sports, vacations and work. Ten minutes would go by and then they each picked up a hamper to go down the wall and check their nets. Once done it was back to the top step and another ten minute wait. On full hamper days they'd pool their catch and sell one hamper to the Lakeview Restaurant down off of Haynes. These earnings became their 'crab fund'. Every six months or so they would take this money and split it down the middle. Sometimes they would talk about taking it and buying a nice wooden skiff; maybe they would even get into the business as real crabbers out on the water. Somehow, though, they both knew it was a bit of a dream and that, more than likely, the other hours of their lives would prevent it.

The years slowly went by and then one morning while checking the nets the conservative had a stroke and died. He keeled over head-first into the water with his hamper in his hand. The liberal tried preserving the memory of his dead friend by going out to the seawall alone. But he was lonely with just the gulls and the sea. He appreciated his talks with himself but they weren't the same. His wife begged him not to go anymore, she believed he was ill. A few months later he was killed in an automobile accident. His picture was in the obituary section for two days, at the end of which time, he was put into the ground.

The seawall looked bare without them, the gulls acted as if they expected their arrival. The young oak continued to grow into a good, solid tree. The bottom step was again run over with algae where once there existed a path worn by the soles of their boots. Nature seemed to forget they existed.

    One morning, still in the lamp black of early morning, two men came to the seawall. They appeared to be in their early thirties and the best of friends. Coming to the seawall was a new experience for them. They felt the urge to do some crabbing. If they liked it maybe they would do it on a regular basis. Hopefully, they might catch enough to sell; the extra cash would certainly come in handy. One of them even developed a plan. They'd take eight nets each and space them out ten yards apart and wait ten minutes before checking them. They were bound to catch something.

    It was best to wait until sunrise before putting the nets in the water so they set their hampers down under the tree and sat down on the top step. They chewed some sticks of gum and talked while watching the violet of the coming sun evolve. Their eyes went out over the water as the ever aware gulls swooped in closer while the first rays came inching toward them. The two men looked at one another and recognized something very old, something very familiar about the whole scene.

A CHANCE TO BE TALL

Take me back to the third grade, 1961.
Sister Caroline, rosy cheeks and spectacles
smelling of a musty habit.
She liked me for some strange reason
that I can't fathom or tell.
Sitting by the windows in bright,
unforgettable sunshine,
watching the clock on the wall,
waiting impatiently for a chance to be tall.
A fire drill brought us all outside
standing neatly in line
'next to the belfry
with a recording for a bell,
girls giggling and whispering
boys dreaming of playground glory.
The sun shone, how it shone!
I can never forget,
that light permeates my life
even now,
the clock on the wall above the door,
the one that represented freedom
has turned over ten thousand times
but my shadow is still
there
in the seat by the windows.
Timothy was a likable enough lad,
athletic and tall for his age.
We had noticed that for days
he had not been in our class-
the sunshine beamed off his empty desk
when it was announced

he had been struck by a car
on Prentiss some weeks before.
It was a horrific crash
which Tim was lucky to survive
but now with impaired senses
and a plate to protect his mind.
Months later he was back with us
but his appearance and manner
had significantly changed,
and we being children
could not stand to look in his eyes
for the change was all too obvious.
'Were his eyes made of glass
was his face now a mask?'
He had returned to us
from a foreign place,
a place far beyond our comprehension
and Jesus God, we ignored him
and his pain only deepened,
always sullen and sad
and not there much longer amongst us.
A month or two later we learned
he had eventually died.

That sunshine, my God, that sunshine,
how it beamed off his empty desk.

St. Raphael School, old building and new extension.

DWAYNE MAKES GOOD
(A FOOTBALL STORY)

In the sixth grade at St. Raphael we were not yet old enough to play on the grass fields behind the school gym. That privilege was reserved for the older kids which meant we were relegated to play on the recently blacktopped parking lot between the church and the cafeteria. It was a hard surface that could punish a child's body if he or she took a bad tumble but at least it was somewhat new and maybe just a touch softer than the old concrete it replaced. Sister Martha was our teacher that year, a nun who appeared too young but who had a very nice face, pretty. How those women wore those black habits at the height of summer was beyond me; they truly did suffer for their savior. Sister Martha's habit always smelled musty like it had been taken from a closet where the door hadn't been opened in a very long time. She is fondly remembered for having a sweet disposition, unlike a lot of the nuns at the school who seemed sour for some reason. She had a laugh that was genuine and came from the belly. She laughed a lot as I recall and when she did her cheeks would become rosier. Her cheeks would also glow when something or someone made her angry like Benny Kraxton was wont to do (he had that penchant for making a lot of the Sisters mad). We never liked to see the Sisters angry because that brought up a lot of fear in us kids. This, thankfully, did not happen all that much.

  It was after Mardi Gras, 1963, that Sister noticed palm-sized footballs being thrown around the blacktop at recesses and lunch. They were made of plastic and usually the colors of Mardi Gras, green, purple or gold. It wasn't just one or two of them being thrown but a lot of them. It became common, albeit confusing, to see twenty or thirty go crisscrossing through the air above the playground. The era of throw-away plastic had begun and Mardi Gras throws would forever change; the beautiful glass beads made in Czechoslovakia had been replaced with hard plastic from Japan and Taiwan, the hard and soft rubber balls that were thrown off the floats were replaced with plastic, more colorful ones, and many, many more of them. The plastic footballs had been thrown by the thousands from the floats that year. The playground air was thick with them and before chaos reigned and the authorities that be banned them from the playground, Sister Martha hatched a plan for us to hang on to them a while longer. Bless her heart. She organized a two man team football league for our class. This would help eliminate some of the balls being thrown and hopefully, make it more palatable for the principal, Sister Bernadine, to digest. Just maybe they wouldn't notice how much fun we kids were having playing with them.

How those teams were formed is a bit fuzzy. It may have been that Sister chose the teams but I like to believe that I picked Dwayne myself. Dwayne Plauche was a gangling looking kid with thick glasses, boxcar ears and a perennial crew cut. Not much was known about him because he lived a good seven or eight blocks away from the neighborhood we played in. He was a new kid too but he looked funny and kids being what they are, always picked on the funny looking ones. What we also noticed about him, though, was that if picked on long enough he would display a fiery temper that would cause him to lash out at his tormentors. He could only be pushed so far and most of the time we kids knew just how far to push him. So, for half the year Dwayne was relegated to the intelligentsia of the class. This might strictly have been because of his looks but for whatever reason he was considered a definite outsider. I knew what it felt like to be an outsider. Born with a partial cleft lip I had a scar an inch and a half long on the left side of my mouth and had been called a bunch of names in my youth ranging from 'big mouth' to 'scar face'. I knew what it was to be ostracized because of my looks but I knew there was more to me that what the mirror displayed just like I knew there was more to Dwayne. So it was that he and I became a team that year and a fledgling friendship began.

Sister Martha gathered all of us together on the blacktop and asked each team to pick a name. She also told us there would be eight games total over the course of four weeks; two a week and we would play each other at least once. At the end of these games the two teams with the best records would play for the "Plastic Football Championship of St. Raphael". It was the first year such a game was to be held and more than likely, the last. Dwayne and I stood together with the sun peeking out from behind the clouds. It was a cold day in February and we still had our red, St. Raphael sweaters on. We stared at each other for a while silently until I finally began to speak to him and asked if he had an idea what name our team should have. To my utter surprise he said he did. He said if it was okay with me, that maybe we should be named the Rhinos because he had seen that animal at the Audubon Zoo and saw how strong and powerful it was and that it was good runner for being so large. I thought that made a lot of sense and was a pretty cool name for a football team so Dwayne and I became the 'Rhino's'. I then asked if he knew anything about playing football and he lowered his eyes to the ground and admitted to me in a low voice that he knew a little but that he wasn't too good at it. I really didn't know what to say to him so we had one of those awkward moments between boys when they don't know how to express themselves. I looked around at some of my friends who were paired together as teams and saw them looking over at Dwayne and I. They were snickering and laughing. I looked at the crown of Dwayne's lowered head and told him not to worry, that it was no big deal that in the end there really wasn't much to it; somebody has to throw the ball on offense and the other guy has to catch it. On defense our job was to stop the other team from scoring and you find out who wins by adding up the points. Dwayne looked at me and saw I was serious in my simplistic description which I'm sure he was probably already aware of. It broke the ice between us. He looked at me with some surprise and realized that I was not ashamed to be with him. The Rhinos were going to play and see what we could do.

At first, what we saw the following week wasn't at all pretty and suddenly I had a few pangs of regret, not for allowing myself to be teamed with Dwayne but more for not suggesting we should at least practice a little. That first game we were out of position both on offense and defense. Early on we tried everything and it was clear that Dwayne was relying on me to make decisions regarding the team's play. I had him playing quarterback while I was going out trying to catch balls that were not getting out of the backfield. Each time I returned to the huddle I could see from Dwayne's expression that he was losing confidence so I suggested we switch roles; I would become the QB and he the receiver. On defense I had him rush the passer because I was afraid that if he got burned while defending a long pass his ego might completely deflate. The first few times he rushed the opposing QB he went charging into the backfield without his arms being raised and got burned by the passer faking one way and running around him for big yards or simply sidestepping him and throwing the ball downfield to his receiver. I told him to walk in with his arms raised high and to be ready to move with the QB if he decided to run with the ball and that, under no conditions was he to run at him, that he was not to panic but to move slowly with him but always with his arms up. Dwayne was a quick study when it came to football; as soon as he figured out that what I was telling him was correct it stopped the quarterback being a threat to easily run around him. What it did was to allow me to concentrate on playing the pass and I was able to intercept a few balls and run downfield. On offense I found that throwing the plastic ball around at lunch was completely different than being under the gun during a game. What became clear to me was that the only way to get the ball downfield was to take something off of it. What this meant was that you didn't throw it hard, that you threw it like a change-up in baseball, a throwing motion governed by slow to medium speed. When I did this it went much further and could even get a tight spiral on the ball. I actually began to enjoy throwing the small ball and what was even more amazing not only to me but to anyone else watching the Rhinos play was that Dwayne Plauche, as a pass receiver was displaying a tenacity and adroitness for the game that few people, including myself, thought he had. He literally tried hard on every pass. Those first few wounded ducks that weren't even close to him were still clawed at while he tried to make his way to the uncatchable arcs of those balls. It was crystal to everyone except Dwayne that the balls weren't going to be caught but he tried anyway. Sometimes perception and image are somewhat misleading; Dwayne didn't look like a football player with those glasses and ears but when this dorky looking kid went out for a pass he became a football player; he was a demon pass receiver with those long arms of his. You have to want it and Dwayne did, badly. By the end of that first game Dwayne and I had had grown a little bit into a team. It was a surprise to everyone including us that the Rhinos had won their first game.

There was always something innate about football on a cold, crisp day; it felt natural to throw a long loping pass and have someone run under it and softly snag it out of the air. As much as that feeling applied to Dwayne and I on the day of our first game there is another feeling that applies to football that might pertain to our second game and it is reminiscent of the dreaded spring training or those early practices in August in full pads that was torturous, that when it was so hot you thought you would die inside the oven of a helmet; then toss in those dreaded end-of-practice wind sprints that lasted so long that if you would have been seen by paramedics they would have had you on IV's pumping as much fluid as they could get into you. During those times there was no place to hide, as much as you felt like the uniform gave you some anonymity, it didn't, and certainly not from the coaches who you swore had eyes wrapped around the circumferences of their heads. That was somewhat the feeling I had during the Rhinos second game; everything was a chore to the nth degree. More than likely that first game and its outcome had lulled us into a false sense of whom and what we were; namely, a gawky kid who had never been part of the group and a sometime athlete who probably lacked the dedication and determination to be first-string on any team. That first game swelled our balloon and we rose high into the air, weightless and full, but the string that ties us to earth was about to be pulled and we would soon rediscover gravity and again, the hardness of the planet's surface.

      Nothing went right. The passes I threw were either off target completely or they were bouncing off Dwayne's hands that seemed to have as much feeling in them as loose rocks in the street. It was funny at times but it was becoming somewhat of a dire situation with the other team intercepting passes and running for touchdowns. I became so deflated that stopping them didn't seem to make much sense. The outcome seemed certain. It was the Colts who had punctured our balloon; John Galla and A.J. Luna could run like the wind that swirled papers around on the blacktop and they were running circles around us. These two were real football players and played like they had just come off the practice field. They were fairly short and although Dwayne and I had the height advantage we could not put it to good use. They beat us with speed and intelligence that came from their young experience and our almost complete inexperience. The Colts knew where to be on almost every play while Dwayne and I were still figuring out exactly what to do which meant we were always a step or two behind. By the end of the game we were fairly close to being competitive with them but the outcome was assured with a three touchdown lead. I believe both of us felt as if the game shouldn't end, that we had left something out on the field that day and although that in itself is a negative feeling we did come away with a sense of something positive. We were sure we weren't as bad as the score reflected and we were positive we could play better. We hoped that maybe somewhere down the line we might have the opportunity to meet the Colts again and prove that we could 'stay' with them.

Our third game saw us a little tight at first but when our bodies and muscles loosened we played with savvy and determination. We ran a trick play to get on the scoreboard first. I had Dwayne come into the back field after centering the ball and I made like I was going to lateral to him and then go out for a pass. Both defensive players bit on the fake and I simply ran around right end for the touchdown. After that I was a threat to run out of the backfield on almost every play. This allowed Dwayne some breathing room out in the secondary. There were times he was so wide open that it seemed like no one was guarding him. He ran for a couple of scores after making some juggling catches. On defense we played well enough to stop them most of the time. We did not hold them scoreless but when the score was close in the middle of the game we were at our best defensively and held them a few times, forcing punts and then breaking the game open with a few interceptions that were run back for TDs. When Sister blew her whistle marking the end of lunch and our game we had won easily. Dwayne and I walked back to class somewhat satisfied but we knew not to get overconfident; we knew we had to play smarter if we were going to win games. More importantly, though, as soon as this game ended we were ready to come back and play the next one, we couldn't wait to get back out there and play. In any team sport that feeling of anticipation for the next contest, the next practice session, the next time you just pick up the ball makes not just the individual better but makes the team better. The Rhino's learned all this as the games went on and we didn't lose that enthusiasm; we stayed focused when on the blacktop playing- we bobbed, we weaved, we adjusted when things weren't going well and we found what worked and as a result we won out. We went unbeaten in the remaining games.

What also became amazingly clear as time went on was that because Dwayne and I developed as a team and won those games against fairly stiff odds we began attracting attention from a lot of kids that were otherwise docile in nature and not on a lot of sixth graders radars. Could this all be due to a small plastic football thrown form Mardi Gras floats that year? There was a certain feeling when all this was taking place that's as lucid now as it was during those weeks when we played. The Rhino's represented what most people would like to do with their lives on any athletic field; succeed against tremendous odds. Dwayne and I weren't supposed to win any games because on the one hand you had a kid who was considered a geek in looks and nature and myself who although had come from a very athletic background had not yet excelled on any athletic field. Our spirits would not accept this and as Rhino's our spirits manifested themselves physically into success and confidence not only on the black top but also in the classroom. We attracted this attention because we were the quintessential underdog. Kids who seemed to have very little hope of ever winning anything on a football field saw themselves Rhinos, like us. For the younger kids we were a sign of hope that maybe one day they too might go out with a chance of winning the game with a juggling, one-handed catch, accomplished while adjusting their glasses during the pass route much like Dwayne sometimes had to do. We became the embodiment of their hopes. They saw us out there and knew there was a chance; there would always be a chance for them and us to succeed.

It was amazing to think just how far we had come from those first few games. Dwayne and I had certainly jelled as a two-man team. We had come into our own and won respect from the kids on both sides of the aisle, even the ones that frowned on us before. What was indeed fascinating and exciting for us was the attainment of the final and championship game and the inevitable rematch with the Colts. We'd be staring into the hard, competitive eyes of A.J. and John; the lean and the quick, the gifted and the beautiful and the darlings of the 'in' crowd. For these two, the epitome of what everyone referred to as 'naturals', everything came effortlessly, easy and they knew it, they felt it; they were super-confident and believed in themselves and felt that games would always go their way. They exuded the attitude. Dwayne and I had a week to the game and everything that I had been thinking and feeling began to chip away at what confidence our wins had afforded us. They had beaten us once and as I mulled that first meeting over I sensed that even if Dwayne and I played to the very best of our abilities and made zero mistakes it might not be enough to overcome them. Colt touchdowns could come by the hamper-full.

    A day or two of tentative thinking usually gives way to panic, then hysteria and then to the final and most ugly stage; fear. I actually became afraid. What froze me was the sobering realization of what this impending game was doing to Dwayne and whatever fragile confidence and self-esteem he might have garnered in the past weeks triumphs. It was as if those games we had won to get here was nothing but a fading memory, a series of silly dreams that you remember for a while when first waking but that quickly vanish later during the clutter of the day. We could barely recall those wins now and whatever intensity of emotion they produced at that time had long since evaporated like the correct ingredients for a gumbo on a gumbo type of day. Dwayne and I winced every time someone patted us on the back and said, "good going, can't wait" and "good luck playing the Colts". For a while Dwayne and I went through a phase where we blamed each other for the present predicament, then we blamed Sister for thinking up such a ridiculous idea: plastic football league, who in their right mind would conjure up such a crazy idea. While we were at it we blamed the world for giving birth to us, for bringing us all this long way through such a complicated series of events that would culminate in our sorry demise against the Colts. It was highly unlikely that we would win, it was more likely that we would be ground into the asphalt of the parking lot. We tried tossing the ball around just to stay focused for the big day but the more we tried to practice the more comical we became. Our fear dictated our entrance onto the Bozo show- football players?- better off running away to clown school. At practice the day before the game I don't believe Dwayne and I had completed a pass or run the correct route to be in position to catch the ball. We stunk that much. Our heads were not in it and our hearts were unsure and obscured by doubt and fear. A.J. and John probably sensed it and swaggered all the more, they even snickered whenever they passed us in the hall as if to say, "y'all don't belong here, anybody but you".

    This game really defined the chasm between the 'have's and the have not's' in our classroom. As I look back I realize that differences like these exist in every school and classroom even now and probably have existed for as long as human beings gather in a collective setting. The bold and the beautiful had to cheer for the Colts; people like Kim Chaplain, head of the Cherub cheerleader squad with perfect skin, beautiful lamp-black hair and big, blinking brown eyes. One reason she had to cheer for the Colts was that she had a crush on A.J. since the first grade. People like Penny Heard, who had brown hair past her waist and such smooth facial skin that Michelangelo would have trouble matching it in carved stone; or like Jimmy Kilgallon, best friend to John Galla and the other wide receiver on the schools 85 pound football team named the St. Raphael Cherubs. These people cheered the Colts on naturally. Who they considered un-natural or that didn't belong were the people cheering for us; people like Karen Lamkin who had a thick coating of soft downy black hair on her arms and the back of her hands; she had been tagged with 'chimp' by the 'have's'. Then there were the Widmer twins who acted so crazy at times that everyone thought there was too much gray matter missing from between their ears. Years later when I ran into them they had not seemed all that different. It didn't matter- I always liked them. Every 'four eyes' in the parish of St. Raphael, it seemed, were cheering for us. It undoubtedly had something to do with the fact that Dwayne wore glasses while running out for passes. The game had drawn people into two distinct camps but I always secretly believed that God cheers for the botched and the bungled; for the improbables. If that were so then God was about the take the spread and bet the Rhino's. So it was on a late day in March, 1963, that the one-and-only plastic football championship of St. Raphael's was to be played. The day dawned crisp and cold and it was one of those immaculately blue sky kind of day that even one cloud looks out of place whether directly overhead or flattened on the horizon. When you're that age it is hard to take your mind off of yourself long enough to notice events like the weather or the news but certain personal events will forever embed themselves in your mind. I'm sure that as Dwayne and I rode our bikes to school on this particular morning it was hard not to think of what lay ahead of us at the lunch recess and our bells felt as if they already had been rung long before the one that signaled the beginning of our school day. I distinctly recall the chill in the morning air and the cold touch of the metal bike rack after pulling my bike into the nearest available slot. It was five minutes from the start of class and I made my way to the room right over the playing area of asphalt where the game would be played a few hours from now. I passed over the parking lot lines that would be our boundaries and recalled how I secretly hoped for time to stand still or at least slow down a bit. As a child my sister and I would play 'time machine' on the swing set in our backyard. I wished someone would tell me that it was yesterday or the day before, any day but this one would be fine with me and probably for Dwayne as well.

The school day began like it had a hundred thousand times before, nothing seemed out of the ordinary except for three plastic footballs that were sitting on Sister Martha's desk. They were green, purple and gold; the traditional Mardi Gras colors. Dwayne and I looked at each other from across the aisles and knew that these were the game balls. Sister had written in black ink across each ball the initials of our school- "SRS." She was ready for the game to be played just like every other person in our class, or for that matter, every sixth grade class in the school as we were soon to find out. But then they were only spectators and for my part I wished for more time, wanted another year or two with my teammate to prepare for the juggernaut that would soon be across the line of scrimmage from us. Ten years might be enough to mold Dwayne and I into real football players. Maybe ten years might be enough but we wouldn't get them, time had run out. What we had was a cold crisp day in March and a noon date with destiny. Even my bright spots weren't all that bright. I thought that because of the weather most kids would stay away from the wide open area of the parking lot where the game was going to be played. On cold days kids had the option of foregoing recess to stay inside the classroom where it was toasty and warm. I fantasized about the entire class coming down with food-poisoning right before the game was to be played and that the teams would be playing in relative obscurity on an empty parking lot. No one would be there to witness our demolition. Or maybe a fire alarm would mysteriously be pulled right before lunch. I wondered if God and luck would be there when we needed them most but all I got back was silence and that was loud enough.

As it was, everything went perfect, the clock didn't stop, the sun rode higher and brighter, some of the chill was taken out of the air and mysteries of all mysteries, the food in the cafeteria was unusually edible that day. As Dwayne and I finished our meal and walked outside under the portico of the new building our mouths dropped open to see not only our entire class ringing the field but almost every other kid from just about every class that used the parking lot at recess lining the field too.

Plastic footballs were whizzing through the air in anticipation of our arrival; the girls that designated themselves cheerleaders were turning cartwheels on both goal lines. As Dwayne and I walked forward a sea of faces parted to allow us entry onto the playing surface. A.J. Luna and John Galla waited there with Sister M at mid-field holding the three balls and beaming a rosy smile. Her cheeks were red with the crispness of the air and the satisfaction of seeing everyone so orderly for the final game. She and Sister Caroline seemed to have their own personal rivalry going as to who had the better class participation but seeing Sister C's class surrounding the field swelled Sister Martha up with pride like some stout penguin who had just gained entrance to the Arctic Circle for life. She knew she had reached us and was a good teacher after all and if that wasn't enough, the vacant athletic director's job at Tulane University awaited. She tossed one of the balls to each team and had us bow our heads. She said a prayer thanking the Almighty for this day and asking his blessing on this crowd and the teams that were to participate in this somewhat unorthodox athletic endeavor. When the prayer ended the most beautiful event occurred, a demure girl with red hair stepped forward and in a melodic voice as crisp as the air began to sing the National Anthem; the lyrics that she didn't quite know were filled in with appropriately hummed notes. The silence that fell over the playground was deafening. Somehow, intrinsically, Dwayne and I both knew that years from this day we would be looking back and remembering. We had accomplished something that no one, not even ourselves believed could be done. It didn't make a difference if we won or lost this game. It would be great and an apt end to our year of improbability but the fact that we were standing in the middle of this asphalt field with the attention of so many upon us was enough to sustain our faith in humanity, ourselves and God. We believed in hope and would henceforth, always believe. If they tell you it can't be done it just isn't so. As her song ended a collective cheer went up from the people ringing the playing surface. I remember looking at Dwayne just then and seeing the wonderment in his blinking, gray eyes. I felt an immense pride that we were both here to feel this excitement. It was the best I had felt in some days and from Dwayne's glance at me I knew he was feeling the same.

  The coin was flipped by Sister M and it may have been a Rex Parade doubloon as they were being thrown for the first or second time by the krewe that year. It seems appropriate because the game was being played with a parade throw. The Rhino's won the toss and as Dwayne and I dropped back to receive I reminded him that this was just a football game, that because there were people standing around watching by what to us seemed like the hundreds, it didn't mean it was any different from the other games we had played in. Yeah, right! We silently agreed to just try and play ball like we've been playing it.

  The kick came my way and Dwayne ran interference down the field hoping to disrupt their coverage. It went like it had in the past, I caught the ball and ran downfield with it. Neither one of us was fast enough to run a kick back all the way for a score unless it was against an exceptionally slower opponent. The Colts definitely weren't one of those. So we set up shop on our end of the field and proceeded to run the plays that had gained us some success in the past; Dwayne would do five or ten yard down-and-outs or across the middle routes. Occasionally, we would run a comeback play where Dwayne would hike the ball and come back in the backfield with me and take a lateral to either run of pass the ball while I scooted into the defensive secondary. Our offensive strategy was not so much flash-and-dance as it was patience and getting the three completions you needed in order to get first downs all the while moving the ball downfield to a hopeful score. Our methods were working, Dwayne ran some good routes and I threw some good passes. We crossed over mid-field which for us was marked by the small, rectangular windows that were high up on the rectory side wall. The glass was smoked and on bright days they resembled mirrors; on this day the sun beamed off them like car headlights on high beam. We converted our first series into one first down, then another. We were on their end of the field when Dwayne caught another pass to move within sight of their goal line. It was here that the Colts called a time-out and huddled. Dwayne came back to me and we waited while A.J. and John talked it over with their arms on each other's shoulders. We could see that they were pumping each other up in an attempt to stop our scoring threat. They came out of their break whooping and hollering like cowboys finishing a cattle drive. The adrenaline rush this provided them worked, their coverage on Dwayne tightened up and my passes had to be low and away so that they wouldn't be intercepted. Before we knew it we were staring at a fourth down near their goal-line and our first important decision of the game had to me made. Do we go for it or punt which in this case meant calling a punt and throwing the ball out of bounds before their goal-line so that they would be pinned down deep in the shadow of their own end-zone. Me? I wanted to play the percentages, the slow methodical game; the one where you took as few chances as possible while relying on your abilities to wear down your opponent. The obvious problem with this was that we weren't going to wear this team down; they would always come back at us clawing and scratching. Besides, they had way more talent than us.

Dwayne was content to let me captain the ship and I knew that whatever decision I made that he would support it. But he raised his eyebrows a bit when I signaled to the other team that we were going for it and not punting. I guess he was a bit surprised but then he may have felt like me in that we were not going to get anywhere against this team by playing the percentages.

In our huddle Dwayne stood in front of me with his back to the line of scrimmage and waited for the play. I told him to run his down-and-out pattern on the left side of the goal-line so that he was just behind the line before his momentum was to take him across the side line and that if he was open I'd get the ball to him; and if not, then I would fake the throw and try to run around A.J. into the end zone. We clapped our hands and broke for the line of scrimmage. Dwayne took the ball right at the middle of the field to snap it and on hut two tossed the ball back to me and ran a deliberate pattern straight at John until he was a step or two behind the goal-line. John took a step backwards at first but when Dwayne reached the goal-line he came up tight on him. Dwayne almost had to push him off to make his cut towards the side line; he did everything he was supposed to do; made his head-fake and cut; the only thing was, John anticipated the play perfectly and wasn't fooled at all by the fake. He stepped in front of Dwayne as he began his lateral move towards the side line. Instinctively, I knew that if I attempted that throw there was a good chance John would intercept it and take it back for a quick six. At that precise instant my other option became reality. A.J. being the good player he was had no knowledge that John had the play read because he was concentrating on me and not looking back at his team-mate. He was intent on trying to block a pass if it was to be thrown. I kept my eyes on Dwayne the whole time the play was emerging but with my peripheral vision I could see that A.J. was following my eyes as they looked out on Dwayne and he was moving in the direction that he thought the ball was going to be thrown from. He was already beginning to time his leap in an attempt to block the pass. My arm went back in the throwing motion and as it did so A.J. scrunched down and was ready to leap like a spring. As my arm came forward he left his feet. A.J. was completely fooled by the fake and didn't have a prayer in Hell of catching me. (Please excuse the language, Sister M)

    Our option play had begun beautifully. By all rights Dwayne and I should have been on the scoreboard first but there was a superior athlete on the blacktop this day that should never be overlooked. When John saw Dwayne had no chance of catching the ball; in fact Dwayne had his feet very close to the side line before I pulled the ball down to make my run, he began a slow drift back toward the middle of the field so that when I put what I thought was the supreme fake on his team mate, A.J., he had a real chance of catching me before I could cross the goal line. With the same peripheral vision I used on A.J. I now could sense failure as I saw John sprinting at me from the other side of the field. I steepened my angle toward the goal line in an effort to get to the line before John could get to me but right before I was to see my foot touch the imaginary line I felt a slap on my left shoulder as John whizzed by me. There was no argument, he had got to me first and now the Colts had the ball for the first time in the game. Dwayne came over to me and apologized. I told him that it wasn't his fault I couldn't outrun John into the end one. I thought it was a good call and an honest-to-God real effort at getting on the board first but the truth was, it did affect us and we played like it. Our minds wandered and we both probably dwelled too long on the missed opportunity. The Colts, of course, used it to their advantage. They moved swiftly down the field with precision passes and well-run routes. With the same adroitness they displayed in stopping us they now employed to drive and score. It was accomplished by a perfect fake that John had thrown at me in the secondary. I froze as he went by my and saw the perfectly thrown pass arc over my head and never bothered to turn to see if Galla had caught it; I knew he had. It seemed that within seconds we had gone from being ahead in this important game to being behind; we were left wondering if there was any way we could beat these guys. At the present we seemed to be a half-step behind both mentally and physically.

  As Dwayne and I stood on our end of the field awaiting the kickoff I thought how ironic it was for me to be on the short end of the score by a team with the name, Colts. My favorite NFL team at the time was the Baltimore Colts and their future Hall-of-Fame quarterback, Johnny Unitas. Johnny U epitomized the position of quarterback on any football team with his passé styled, high-topped cleats and his classic over-arm throwing motion. Whenever I saw those cleats and crew-cut hair style I thought about my father who played in the league during the mid-1940's. In those days the helmets were made of hardened leather and there were no face masks to protect you. My father once told me that he had broken his nose eleven times throughout his playing career. He wasn't lying; the line of his nose resembled a curvy rural highway in some old road atlas. Unitas was a pure pocket passer who, if his protection broke down, looked like an old bowlegged cowboy running towards the side line. When he was forced to run out of the pocket the crowd sent up a moan. But when his protection was good and he had time to throw the ball his delivery of the ball was the most beautiful throwing motion you would ever see. It was pure perfection, poetry. Standing there on that goal line being scored upon by a team named the Colts was hard but the thought of Johnny U inspired me. Anything was possible, even beating this team and if not that then at least making a competitive game of it. This thing wasn't over; there was still a lot of game to be played. We received the kickoff and made our customary five or ten yards returning it. In order to build some confidence we ran a few short pass routes, the kind that are almost impossible to defend as long as the ball is snapped quickly and the routes short enough. The game can be about how quickly one can get rid of the ball. The only problem with this strategy is that after two completions the defense knows that you will be throwing short again in order to get the third completion for the first down and a new series. There might be times when you have the tendency to not even take a step downfield but instead pass the ball as soon as it is hiked in order to get that first but the rule is that you at least have to be beyond the present line of scrimmage. We marked that point by designating someone to stand on the sideline and be the marker. Our designee for this game was Jimmy Kilgallon or Kills for short. He was red haired lanky kid whose tennis shoes always looked in need of a wash. He had a big smile on his freckled face, obviously elated to be chosen the marker for the game because we had kids clamoring to be that designee. For them, it was an honor to be part of it and besides, it was one of the best seats in the house for viewing the action up close. This had turned out to be our version of the grown-up game and it really meant something to all of us. Viewed from a distance it must have truly been an intriguing sight, all these kids standing around a small rectangular surface watching four kids toss a tiny lime colored plastic ball to each other, desperately leaping and running after it. In essence, though, that's what any athletic endeavor is about; tossing and catching a ball of some type. The meat on this bone is exactly how it is tossed and caught.

   The ball was snapped and Dwayne ran a perfect little buttonhook pattern in the middle of the field and I threw the ball right at his belt buckle so there was no chance for John to intercept it or block it. When Dwayne looked over at Kills to see where the line of scrimmage was we could see that it was a completion by a couple of feet. The Colts watched as Kills took a step toward their goal-line to mark the new line of scrimmage. The Rhinos weren't going to lay down and die, we had come too far for that but by no means did Dwayne and I get too cocky because we knew what the Colts were capable of and the scoreboard never lies; we were still behind. The new set of downs did put some badly needed wind into our top sails. We ran more short plays and scraped out another series before the Colts woke up and put an end to our mini-march downfield. On the next series we completed only one short pass and then punted the ball away to the Colts. We watched as they huddled and prayed not be run over by this young herd of ponies. With our confidence again on the wane, the Colts read our minds and used our option strategy against us. On first down they decided to run the ball. On a quick snap John sprinted out straight at me, gave a head fake left and shot for the right side line. Having taken the fake in stride I was shoulder-to-shoulder with him as we went across the field. Before I made my customary glance back towards the quarterback, I sensed something was wrong. It was one of those frozen seconds when an eternity seems to pass and you feel as if you are sitting at the window of a train about to derail. The telltale sign was in John's eyes, or rather, in the direction that John's eyes were aimed. Any receiver worth his weight would have been looking back for the ball but John wasn't. His eyes were straight ahead, almost as if he were intent on keeping my eyes from glancing back for as long as possible. Of course he did not want me looking back toward the quarterback because the quarterback was off-and-running.

  A.J. had taken the snap and stared ahead looking for his receiver. On long pass plays it was customary for the quarterback to hold the ball for as long as possible to allow the receiver to get to this intended mark downfield. Sometimes, a QB would have to take a few steps back in order for this to occur. A.J. took those steps which once done cancels the 'walk-in rule'. The 'walk-in rule' in touch football was that the defender must always walk, albeit at a brisk pace, towards the quarterback until he takes a step either way out of the protected bubble of the pocket; once that happens then the rusher can now truly run at the passer. A.J.'s movement caused Dwayne to begin a full-fledged sprint at him hoping to time a leap to either deflect the pass or obstruct A.J.'s view downfield. As soon as Dwayne left the solidity of the St. Raphael black-top he could probably hear my voice inside his head reminding him never to run at the quarterback unless he runs first and that includes if he just takes a step away from the pocket. He was also probably feeling the same sick to your stomach sensation that I was feeling. At the instant Dwayne left the ground A.J. vanished around him and was on his way downfield with me mired in trickery and molasses on the other sideline with Galla. By the time I changed direction he was running flat out towards our end zone.

When you're young your instincts are tuned to your reflexes. A.J. had these attributes but then so did Dwayne and I. In a race where both competitors have the same youthful reflexes, pure speed is the determining factor. I'd lose a fifty yard sprint to John by a couple of steps, this was a certainty but in a similar race with A.J. I'd have the advantage and luckily this was the scenario we were now presented with. I was instinctive enough to reverse my field and begin sprinting at him as soon as I saw him leave the backfield. I took the right angle and put the customary slap on his right shoulder some five yards from our endzone but the speed I had to generate took me flying out of bounds where luckily with so many kids watching the game that they prevented me from falling on the hard surface of the asphalt. Actually, Kim Chaplin and Pat McDonald were the two I massaged the most while flying willy-nilly across the sideline. They caught me with their arms and slowed me down. There's nothing like making a good defensive play and getting massaged by two of the cutest girls in the class at the same time.

A play like that would usually set a chain of events in motion that would spell defeat for the weaker team. They would go back to the line of scrimmage confused and tired after being faked out and almost scored upon. They would not be athletically prepared for the next play and standing there would be dictated to as far as the course of the game that ensued was concerned. A score on the next play or two would seem almost inevitable. Having played organized ball and street ball up the wazoo I knew that would be the case and the only way to stop it is to take a breather and try to interrupt the flow of the game, a flow that was more like a strong current that Dwayne and I found ourselves swimming against. The Colts were eager to snap the ball, they smelled victory but before they did I called a time out and Dwayne and I walked back into our endzone to take a breather.

We stood there, off to one side and looked at each other and shook our heads slowly from side-to-side. Strange how at certain times in life you find the need to say absolutely nothing because what truly needs to be said is being imparted by expression, by gesture and by attitude. Sometimes it can even be said by the scene around you. Dwayne and I were silently apologizing to each other. We had become friends and friends know when and how to apologize. We realized, though, that it wasn't so much our failure as it was a testament to their athletic ability. These two guys were good, not just physically on the field but mentally as well. We felt close to them in these areas but harbored no illusions about being better than them. However, the old cliché, 'on any given Sunday anybody can win', somehow rang true to us. We just didn't know if that day happened to be this day but we knew we had to stick around long enough to find out. The evolution of the Rhino's was fueled by the belief that we were better than what the Colts thought we were; and that we could always play better. "Play better, play better" became our mantra and we chanted it on the way back to the line of scrimmage.

With our attitudes adjusted the Colts prepared to snap the ball on second down. As soon as the ball was snapped the Colts went into motion and John again led me to the other side of the field only this time I knew what was coming and decided to play off of him a little. Dwayne walked steadily into the backfield with his long arms extended and kept his eyes focused on A.J.'s hips. Dwayne was not going to leave his feet and leap at A.J. again no matter what he did and when A.J. saw this he threw a pass fake at him and tried to go around Dwayne anyway. It was half-hearted attempt, though, and Dwayne touched him in the backfield for a big loss. Dwayne looked back at me and smiled. I thought I saw him mouth the chant again, "play better, play better".

They still had two more shots at the end zone and John was going to have to catch passes if they were going to score so I knew I was going to have to be there right next to him if I was going to have a chance to properly defend the passes thrown his way. On third down he went for the left corner of the end zone and I was right there with him. When he looked back for the ball I looked back as well and found it right over my head headed straight for his outstretched hands. My right arm went up and knocked it away. On fourth down they tried a pass option. A.J. ran to the right side and John went out and into the end zone on the same side so that both QB and receiver are moving in the same direction as the pass is thrown. It is a timing play that everything has to be just right in order for it to work; a hard enough thing to accomplish under normal conditions, never mind that we were playing with a plastic ball no bigger that the palm of your hand. The margins for success get as small as the ball. A.J.'s running motions seemed to influence the balls flight as soon as it left his hand. He was running fast so the ball sailed too high and long. Not being very tall to begin with, John leaped in vain at the pass. His outstretched arms came nowhere close and their scoring threat was stopped. At least for a while Dwayne and I proved that we could 'play better'.

We knew we had to carry over that firm resolve to our offensive scheme but our hopes were somewhat dampened to find that the Colts stepped their game up a notch too. Both sides got serious and any laughter or smiles disappeared for a while. For the next few series the defenses prevailed and it seemed that any offensive gain was impossible, not only that, but an outside factor came into prominence. At times the playground could act like a wind tunnel that would funnel soft breezes into gale like gusts; sometimes in the late afternoon sun the wind would be ripping through your hair and make it impossible for some of the girls to keep their scarves or beanies on while departing church. If the wind was kicking up like that it was extremely difficult to govern the flight of that Mardi Gras trinket. Everything could be rolling along fine and then for some unknown reason, for who can predict when the wind will blow and how hard; on a random play, you just had to hope that it wasn't a crucial play, the wind would catch a ball in mid-flight and knock it down or completely reverse its direction. If it hadn't meant so much to us it would most definitely be slapstick comedy at its finest. There were plays when both teams were scrambling around for balls of uncertain direction like loose change being dropped among thirsty people at a soft drink machine. You'd think at times like these it would be better to run the football but with just two man teams the running game was too predictable and boorish which translated into very little offense and very few scores.

What this meant was that time was running out for the Rhino's. The lunch recess was less than an hour long and with most of that time being consumed eating lunch we didn't have but thirty or forty minutes to play on the playground. We were fighting the elements, the clock and the scoreboard. We needed a quick TD but the steel curtain of defense that the

Colts had thrown up was zapping our strength; not to mention our confidence. It's at times like these that chance comes into play, when freak luck rears either its beautiful or ugly head, depending on your perspective. For Dwayne and me, two altar boys playing next to a church, the beautiful, exceptional head of luck made its poetic appearance. For A.J. and John, also two altar boys, it's my guess they would have preferred to have been home watching TV when freak luck chose to raise its grotesquely ugly face.

'Tripping over your own feet' is usually a cliché that applies to the lazy and the uninspired. To mention this phrase in the presence of a gifted athlete like John Galla was a misnomer. When freak luck shows up, however, everyone is at risk no matter your talents. We had succeeded once more in stopping the Colts on an offensive series and they were preparing to punt to us again. Dwayne and I were taking our usual positions to field the punt and we were in a bit of a trance-like state with nothing much happening in this stalemate of a game when as I saw John hurtling at me full speed something truly amazing happened. I was meandering towards this human bullet aimed at me when I decided, by instinct, as if something good might come of it, to stop dead in my tracks. When I did, the look on Galla's face as he felt his own feet tangle beneath him was painful even for me to watch. He could not stop himself from falling or correctly put, from free-falling. It made me wonder what the playing field looked like from his view, considering I had not fallen yet and seen all those faces standing around hovering above me. Besides, the asphalt was somewhat hard and it could take the skin off your hands and knees quickly and painfully. If that happened, weeks could go by before you could start picking the scabs off those quasi-healed wounds. The thing was, Galla guessed that I would be going to my right after my dead stop and the best he could do was to fall in that direction and pray that he had guessed right so that an outstretched arm might find me and down me before any further damage could be done. Dwayne was downfield taking A.J. with him when he heard me call out his name. To his credit he knew he had to get behind me while running a parallel course because at the same time Dwayne saw me so did A.J. and he was on the same side of the field that I was now on.

A.J. had the line to catch me but he would have to leave Dwayne alone to do it and he now knew that John wouldn't be able to help him. He could plainly see his teammate down on the asphalt and completely out of the play. So A.J. did the only thing he could do. He came directly for me but right before the touch came I flipped that beautiful plastic ball sideways to Dwayne who grasped at it with both hands and took it the rest of the way into the endzone. It was definitely one of those plays that occurs in the blink of an eye and which usually affects the outcomes of big games. This one was to be no different.

Before A.J. and John could collect their wits we ran a down-and-out pass play that not only decided the extra point but the rest of the game as well. Dwayne was not open on the play. John had him covered so that any pass I threw in front would be picked off or knocked away. What this meant was that I had two choices; either throw the ball completely away so no one had a chance to catch it or throw the ball high over their heads and hope Dwayne with his height advantage could somehow come down with it. The ball was thrown three feet above his head and I honestly believed it was way too high for him to catch but he timed his leap perfectly and launched into the air to pull it down with both hands. John had to be feeling deflated with falling down on the previous play and now not being able to stop the extra point because he simply wasn't tall enough.

After Dwayne caught the extra point I turned and was walking towards our end zone to prepare for the kickoff when I saw the outcome of the game in my mind's eye. It was a strange thing, this prognostication; it produced a feeling of anticipation. I could not wait to get my hands on the ball again to test my theory. It occurs to me now that as I look over my life there have been moments when I've experienced this feeling from both the positive and negative poles of perspective. The phrase, 'going with the flow' has captured this feeling perfectly because once this feeling begins to emanate there is little one can do but to flow with it. It is like the proverbial snowball rolling downhill; try to prevent it and you waste your time. Clearly, standing in the surf beating the waves back with nothing but a stick is an act of either senseless desperation or optimism tinged by lunacy.

 As Dwayne reached my side I tuned and put my arm around him and smiled knowingly. He sensed that the Cheshire grin on my face was something more than the fact that we had just scored, but he had confused it with my sense of protocol and his paranoia. He sheepishly looked at the ground while we were walking and asked if his shirt-tail was hanging out or were the glasses sitting straight on his face. I clipped that stray hair by saying he was great, perfect, that there was nothing wrong but that everything might be right with the world, or at least with this world, our world right now on this bright blue winters day. His expression then turned from one of concern to confusion and puzzlement. I looked at him, said that the Rhinos were not going to lose this game and winked. The other amazing aspect to my divining the outcome of the game was Dwayne's faith in me. Right after that wink the look of anticipation over the improbability of us winning that game swept over his face and I knew then that the universal tumblers had just clicked into place.

 As we prepared to kick off we saw Sister Martha dig deep inside her habit and pull out the man's pocket watch she carried to tell her how much time was left for recess. We could see from the skeptical look on her face that little time remained. Quickly, we kicked off and the Colts ran the ball towards us. They were still emotionally timid and we downed them deep inside their end of the field. Then Sister walked over to us with the watch in her hand.

    She was just about to speak when I interjected and pleaded for one more offensive series for both teams. It would give us a chance to determine a winner of this game. Sister Martha's red cheeks stayed pallid and to her credit she listened and decided fairly for a nun. Most nuns seemed trodden on by misplaced emotions and by devilish kids that saw school and nuns as obstacles on their roads to fun; which in the end led some of them to adult playgrounds from which they would rarely return. Luckily, there weren't many kids like that in their classes but one was enough to send these hard working religious women into an angry frenzy that could carry over to the rest of the class. Sister M, I'm sure, would have preferred that no one win this game, that there would be no winner or loser and that this game and all games end in a tie. To her it might have been the perfect solution to the imperfect world. She fixed her gaze on me and since the Colts or Dwayne did not object to my suggestion she tucked the watch back into her deep habit pocket, the one where they also kept their rosaries and whispered okay. There was going to be one more series for each team.

    The Colts huddled deep in their end of the field and as they did Dwayne and I clasped hands and swore there would be no mistakes. "No mistakes", we said and broke our huddle with a loud clap at the exact second the Colts broke theirs. A look of determination and focus was chiseled onto all our faces. When the crowd surrounding the field found out that there was only to be a few more plays they became more vocal, shouts for either team could be heard and they pressed closer to the sidelines to see.

    Their first play was, of course, a short pass to Galla. He took a few steps forward and scooted quickly towards the right sideline; my peripheral vision allowed me to see the ball leave

A.J.'s hand. When the crowd realized the play was coming towards them they gave way and made some room for John and I to finish the play. John caught the ball a step or two from the sideline and went straight out of bounds. A few friends held him from going any further or falling but it was a very small gain.

They went back to their huddle and we to ours. We again voiced our chant, "no mistakes" and broke for the line of scrimmage. As John hiked the ball to A.J. my instincts told me that they had to try for something a little deeper. John threw his customary head fake at me and turned the speed on to get around me. The speed, though, seemed a little slowed, maybe he was thinking about the tumble he took a while ago because he appeared reluctant to turn the after-burners on. Because of that split-second hesitation he wasn't able to shake me. We turned together to pick up the flight of the ball but I was in front and because of that, closer to the ball than he. The ball was mine, all I had to do was grab it with both hands and hold on. John saw this and being the smart player he was, knew he couldn't let that happen. As I reached for the pass John timed his deflection attempt perfectly and slid his arm directly in between mine and knocked the ball away where it hit someone in the crowd and fell to the asphalt with a few plastic thuds.

Dwayne and I re-huddled. Our "no mistakes" chant greeted the Colts when they turned to face the line of scrimmage on third down. The ball was centered and John immediately shot back into the backfield. A.J. lateraled the ball to him and took out on a pass route of his own with Dwayne in quick tow. We had it played nicely although with someone taller it may have had more of a chance for success. As it was, John barely got the ball over my outstretched arms and I swear that I could feel the air brush over my fingertips as the ball cleared them. It was a hurried pass, though, and A.J. did not have time to completely finish running the route.

Neither one of them knew the ball was coming as quickly as it did and as it was, Dwayne happened to be the closer to the hurried throw. In fact, it hit him in the left shoulder and if he would have turned around faster may have had a chance to intercept it but Dwayne was playing smart defense and was not going to turn until A.J. did. When he did all he could do was watch as the ball fell harmlessly to the ground where it rocked a few times until Kills picked it up and walked slowly back to the line of scrimmage with it.

On fourth down the ball was snapped and John took off like a shot, holding nothing back because this was it, this was their last gasp. He went by me like a bullet on the first few yards but I turned it on and was catching up to him fast. I had hoped that the pass had not been thrown but if it was, maybe it was off target and not perfectly aimed. All my wishes went unheard right at that nanosecond. It had been thrown and from what I could see, looked to be thrown on target. It sailed over my head and was last seen descending towards John's racing, outstretched arms. I had an extreme feeling of drowning when freak chance intervened again. The wind gusted and took some revs off the ball but more importantly, pushed it over to the right sideline where John seemed to have no chance at getting to it. He tried valiantly, though, and went down to the ground twisting and turning to get his body back to the ball. It was all for naught. The Colts did not score and the best they could hope for in this game was to stop us and take the tie. But hold on, the Rhino's had four shots at it too and Dwayne and I both had a feeling that our momentum snowball was about to hit a tree and maybe bury the Colts under all that mass.

We took over on downs on our side of the field in approximately the same place the Colts had begun their series. In this manner we had nearly the same yardage to cover that they had. As Dwayne and I stood in our huddle we heard some shouts for us from the sidelines; one came from Pat

McDonald, a slender auburn-haired girl that had thrown a party just a few weeks before. She had asked me to dance and for an eleven year old boy that was a memorable event. I guess I smiled because she was smiling at me when I looked over at her. The kids that were Dwayne's friends finally spoke up and they encouraged him with shouts like, "come on, do it, do it!" or "charge, Rhino's, charge!" Their tone seemed to be one of hopeful victory for the underdogs, us. We had made them dream a little bit and Dwayne had proven to his friends that it might be possible; that among the glittering bikes in the gray steel bike racks and the mini-tornadoes of paper that the three buildings created on the playground that a huge upset was in the making. The 'in crowd' was amazed by this and strangely silent. They no longer knew who or what to cheer for.

It didn't matter; the snowball had not finished gathering mass and speed. What the Colts last play had told us was very important. It had signaled the prevailing direction that the wind was blowing and it was favorable for us; if anything it would enhance the flight of the ball, exaggerate its spin and distance. I sensed that Dwayne's height advantage was the last cog in the gear wheel and that the key to unlocking victory was the wind and how to use it; it was to be that last little bit of mass picked up by that snowball. I looked over and saw a line of pigeons sitting atop the sacristy to the church, below them was Father Mack and Monsignor Aleman standing on the small concrete porch near the back door. They were in a state of half dress for the afternoon mass. They became transfixed onlookers who, no doubt, were amazed by the lack of activity over most of the playground except for this one spot where everyone seemed to be gathered, watching four small children throw a football the color of a lime. The inactivity attracted them at first but it was the sight and sounds of an impromptu sporting event that kept them there now.

Dwayne and I ran a short pass play on first down just as the Colts had done only we were giving them a glimpse of their demise by throwing the ball high and letting John think that it was a muffed play instead of a test to see if Dwayne was going to be able to leap and catch the ball. He did leap but I had mistimed the throw and the ball sailed higher than Dwayne was capable of leaping. The pass fell incomplete some ten yards beyond his jump. I told Dwayne and he agreed that we needed to hide our ruse one more play or we risked the possibility of the Colts figuring out what we were up to. If that happened they would just play deep and prevent any long pass from occurring. We ran a deep down and out on the next play and I threw the ball on a line that was more horizontal than vertical. It was a hard and fast throw. Dwayne and John both reached for the ball at the same time but because John was so fast he was able to touch the ball before Dwayne could get to it and knocked it away. Again the Colts had succeeded in stopping our play. They slapped each other on the back and yelled, "Yeah, yeah" while punching holes in the air with their fists. Their fans clapped and screamed encouragement at them.

Dwayne came back to the huddle and he could tell from the look on my face that it was time to get serious. I told him to hike the ball from his usual position on the field and run his basic short pattern, the ten to fifteen yard buttonhook down the middle of the field and turn around. When he made his stop and turned around I would pump-fake the pass and he, in turn, would proceed downfield, accelerating to a sprint for the end zone. What I had hoped was that Galla whom I knew would be playing off Dwayne, expecting the deep ball would bite on the fake just a little bit and come up some so that Dwayne at least could be even with him downfield when the ball was thrown. It was here that our strategy was critical; if I could throw the ball just high enough to let the wind take it further maybe there was a chance Dwayne could come down with it over the much shorter John.

It was snapped back to me quickly and John was where we thought he would be, some ten of fifteen yards off of Dwayne, already backpedaling; guessing we would probably throw the long ball. Dwayne ran the pattern perfectly. When he made his button-hook downfield I pumped the ball at him and John stopped his rearward motion and began movement back towards Dwayne. That slight hesitation was what we were banking on, without it the play had no chance to succeed. The ball was thrown on the uplifting wings of a favorable wind. It had rolled off my fingers with alacrity which launched it into a hard and tight spiral of a throw. It seemed to be thrown on the preverbal wire right down the middle of the field arcing to the height we hoped it would attain. It was correctly aimed at both of them and they both now were turning to see exactly where the orb was.

  John must have known at that precise second that his mistake would cost him and the Colts dearly. If he hadn't bit on the fake he would have stayed further downfield which meant that even if Dwayne had caught the pass, which he doubted he ever would, he still would have been in position to down him immediately and prevent the winning score. That possibility must have played itself out in John's mind after the game but he also probably consoled himself with the notion that no one was ever going to remember a silly playground game that did not involve coaches and parents and real football venues. However, this written memoir is proof otherwise.

  The precise second had arrived. They left their feet, both perfectly synchronized. At the apex of their respective leaps Dwayne's fingers were probably a foot higher than Johns and it was in these twelve inches that the outcome of the game lay. As the lime colored ball reached them Johns leap had peaked and he was already slightly descending. Dwayne, on the other hand, had not which was great because the wind carried the ball a little higher and his ascent allowed him to barely reach it and take the spin and velocity off its flight by nudging it up a little further but more importantly, forward, towards the Colts goal-line. As it came down John was all done in and Dwayne was there to cradle the ball and skip beautifully into the endzone completely untouched. I ran downfield to congratulate my team mate but his friends had closed ranks around him and the best I could do was reach in and shake a few of his fingers. He saw me, though, and smiled. It is a smile that has stayed with me all these years.

What I took away from the experience was not that a game could change who you are outwardly but that it could touch your spirit and affect you positively on the inside. Dwayne did not become one of the chosen few because of that game; he did not change his appearance and forsake his friends for the 'in' crowd. He stayed pretty much the same but I noticed that he no longer looked at the ground when talking to people, that he looked them straight in the eye and held his head up as if giving them an indication of the true nature of his height. For the rest of that year Dwayne and I remained fairly close friends. We talked a lot and sometimes played together but eventually we drifted apart and resumed our separate but distinct lives. I don't believe that we were ever in the same class again and I know that we went to different high schools. However, whenever our roads did meet we came together like true friends and always shook hands before talking of our friends and families. When we parted it was always with a smile, a smile that showed we had bonded as a team years ago and had accomplished something together that was extraordinary. I hope that wherever he is now that he's happy and successful in his life and I wonder if he recalls that game with the same fondness of memory that I do. Does he recall the year the Rhinos came out of the woods and played in a certain section of the river, how they made it their own for a brief time and then disappeared back into the jungle. It was the year of the purple and gold colored footballs. How could one ever forget?

THE HISTORIC SITES OF GENTILLY

I.
SPANISH FORT ON THE BANKS OF BAYOU ST. JEAN (JOHN)

One of the stone structures rises up from the grass at Spanish Fort.
To the right is reportedly the fenced off grave of Sancho Pablo.

      The term 'Spanish Fort' came into existence during the late 1800's when the patrons of the hotel erected on the site believed that the decaying brick walls were actually the ones erected by the Spanish in 1779. They were, in fact, the walls that the Americans rebuilt prior to the War of 1812 in 1808.

Spanish Fort Timeline

1. 1701- French traders and trappers erect a wooden palisade at the mouth of Bayou St. John two years after Messrs. Iberville and Bienville rediscover the mouth of the Mississippi River.
2. 1789- Spanish Authorities erect the present fort and supply soldiers to man it and cannon to guard it.
3. 1808- five years after Napoleon sells Louisiana to the United States Spanish Fort undergoes a rebuild.
4. 1814- on December 1st Andrew Jackson lands at Spanish Fort to take command of the American Forces prior to the Battle of New Orleans. The fort was manned by some of Jean and Pierre Lafitte's pirates, The Baratarians, in case of a British invasion from south of the city.
5. 1823- the land and fort sold to Harvey Elkins by Act of Congress.
6. 1825- first Pontchartrain Hotel is erected on the site.
7. 1825-1878- fort and land pass through several hands including those of John Slidell, the city of Slidell's namesake.
8. 1878- the site become an amusement park and resort area.
9. 1883- Theater built and houses an opera company for several seasons. Oscar Wilde, the famed British author, lectures here in the later part of the 18th century. Theater eventually burns down and never rebuilt.
10. 1926- Spanish Fort Amusement Park and resort area closes.

The front steps of the fort were reportedly the ones that led up to a hotel on the site.

These walls of Spanish Fort line the banks of Bayou St. John.

This stone structure on the north side of the fort is a mystery. Only reference is that at one time it was a water fountain.

1930's picture of the fort and boats on Bayou St. John.
The walls are in the background.

1930's picture of the front of the fort and hotel steps.

II

The Milneburg Light House

In the early years of the 1820's the Scottish entrepreneur, Alexander Milne purchased 22 miles of Lake Pontchartrain shoreline stretching from Jefferson Parish all the way to the Petit Coquilles, aka- Fort Pike at the Rigolets. Here are the other tidbits on the light house.

1. Early 1820's- Port Pontchartrain becomes the first artificial harbor on the lake.
2. 1831- the Pontchartrain Railroad begins operation. Patrons from the French Quarter and Uptown ride the Smoky Mary out to Milneburg.
3. 1837- first lighthouse is built for $10,000. In 1854, critics described it as an "ugly, wooden octagonal tower". The light is basically a revolving chandelier.
4. 1855- present lighthouse is built on a concrete pad supported by pilings driven into the lake bottom. The lamp is an ultra-modern-day 5th order Fresnel lens.
5. 1860-1865. During the Civil War the Pontchartrain lighthouse is the only one on the Gulf Coast to retain its keeper.
6. 1869- a hurricane destroys the residence, wharf and cistern but the light house survives.
7. 1880-lighthouse height is increased by adding seven feet of new brick which gives it its distinctive dumb-bell appearance.
8. 1882- begins the tenure of three women light-keepers. The most prominent of which is Margaret R. Norvell. She is described as an extraordinarily compassionate woman who performs many acts of kindness and charity for the residents and sailors of Port Pontchartrain.

9. 1903- another hurricane destroys every structure on the lower coast except for the lighthouse and its residence. Ms. Norvell shelters over 200 people until help arrives.
10. 1929- Port Pontchartrain lighthouse is decommissioned.
11. 2013- the US Coast Guard names its newest Fast Response Cutter in honor of Margaret R. Norvell.

Milneburg lighthouse in late 2015.

A view of the lamp room.

Close-up view of the ball and finial atop the lamp room roof.

Another shot of the rail and crown molding of Margaret Norvell's lamp-room.

Early 1900's picture of the residence and lighthouse.

III

Shushan (Lakefront) Airport
&
The Four Winds

Lakefront Airport terminal building, aka- Shushan Airport.
Heavily flavored Art Deco construction interior and exterior.

In the 1920's the site of what would become Lakefront Airport was populated by rickety camps owned by fishermen and crabbers. The president of the Orleans Levee District, Abraham Shushan, envisioned a modern New Orleans which meant an airport to accommodate planes that would one day carry cargo and people to the city from all points beyond. He foresaw an airport built on reclaimed land from Lake Pontchartrain and began the process of trying to acquire the land from the camp owners. After three years of litigation brought by the camp owners the land was acquired and construction of Shushan Airport finally began in 1931. The construction was highlighted by the unique double cement walls that jutted out into the lake. Pictures taken during the construction of these dual walls showed that the space between them was filled with tons of oyster shells dredged from the lake bottom. Once the walls were completed the lake bottom was hydraulically lifted to fill in the area so that hangars and runways could be built. This was done without fear of further litigation because all lake and river bottoms are considered in the public domain. As irony would have it, Abraham Shushan and other members of the Levee Board were convicted of tax evasion and fraud in 1939 and his name removed from the façade of the building. It is thereafter always been known simply as Lakefront Airport. The terminal building is a beautiful example of Art Deco construction carried out by the WPA created under Franklin Roosevelt's administration. The Mexican artist, Enrique Alferez, did the friezes on the front of the terminal building and also created a fountain on the grounds, titled- The Fountain of the Four Winds. It fanned controversy in the conservative environs of 1930's New Orleans due to the fact that Alferez portrayed the Winds as three women and one man totally in the nude. It is stated that at some point Alferez took to protecting the artwork at night armed with a rifle because of threats that they would be blown up. The controversy was eventually put to rest by Roosevelts wife, Eleanor, who decreed the statues should remain intact and not be touched. Alferez also created the "Girl on a Dolphin" in the pond of the rose garden in City Park and a few other pieces around the park.

TIMELINE OF SHUSHAN AIRPORT

1. 1922- Abraham Shushan pushes for a Lakefront improvement project that would cost $15 million dollars which would include $4 million for an airport. Governor Huey Long backs the proposal.
2. 1928-'31- camp owners sue to block Shushan's project.
3. 1931- litigation over, construction of the airports dual walls begins.
4. May 20th, 1932 first pile for the buildings driven.
5. June, 1932- first plane lands at airport.
6. November 1, 1933- Shushan Airport officially opens.
7. 1934- Pan-American Air Races held at airport.
8. 1936- Works Progress Administration beautification project begins. $250,000 invested for extensive landscaping, paving roads and runways and artwork.
9. 1938- Mexican artist, Enrique Alferez creates his "Fountain of the Four Winds".
10. 1939- Abraham Shushan convicted of tax evasion and fraud. Sent to prison and although eventually pardoned by Harry Truman, his name is removed from the airport façade and renamed Lakefront Airport.

Double wall construction of Shushan Airport. Oyster shells dredged from the bottom of the lake fill the middle space. 1931.

The Art Deco sculpture on the façade of the Lakefront Airport terminal building.

The compass rosette on the lobby's terrazzo floor.

Enrique Alferez's Fountain of the Four Winds.

The serene face of the East Wind. Fountain of the Four Winds, Lakefront Airport.

EPILOGUE

First, I apologize for omitting that certain something, someone or some place that you felt should absolutely be included in a book on Gentilly. Memory is a funny thing but purely a subjective matter and I'm sure that your memories are as poignant as mine are concerning this great area that we knew. Most of these stories were written over twenty years ago when they were still somewhat fresh in my mind. Some, however, were written nearly 40 years ago when I still lived in the area.

I wrote the book because of my great love and respect for the area. I also believed that its history should be told. Although it is true that the Gentilly I knew has mostly vanished the reality is that it's still there as a constantly evolving chapter of the story that is New Orleans. I don't know about y'all but I have great memories of coming out on a Fourth of July night and watching the fireworks over Pontchartrain Beach or coming out of an all-afternooner at the Pitt and going over to the Milneburg snowball stand and slurping down five cent snowballs or taking my bike to St. Raphael and stopping at Messina's Sweet Shop on Marigny to get a Hubigs. Those were indeed the days my friends. My hope is that when you read these you will feel the nostalgia cover you like a warm blanket on a Chilly Gentilly night. I know some might seem a bit maudlin, a bit corny, a bit sickly sweet but I still have dreams about the house I was raised in. I still have dreams about walking across the wide neutral ground of Elysian Fields. I still dream about Gentilly and its people so yes, Gentilly is forever on my mind.

CREDITS

Chilly Gentilly was gleaned from many different sources.

1. John Smith Kendall- "History of New Orleans". Kendall was a professor at Tulane University in the early 1920's and published his 700 page history of the city in 1922. It is still of particular relevance today.
2. Grace King- "New Orleans: The Place and the People". King was a well-known historian of New Orleans and Louisiana. Her book was published in 1895.
3. J.H. De Grange- Historical Date of Spanish Fort. Jan-Oct, 1917.
4. Darby's History of Louisiana, John Mellish, Philadelphia, 1816.
5. Genteel Beginnings by Ned Hemard.
6. Preservation Resource Center of New Orleans.
7. The Louisiana Division Collection of the New Orleans Public Library.
8. Teresa Thessen, "New Orleans Lakefront Airport," New Orleans Historical.
9. Wikipedia and searches that related to New Orleans and Gentilly.
10. New Orleans Churches.com. Site designed by John and Kathleen DeMajo.

In addition pictures and resources were used from the Louisiana State Museum Collection and The New Orleans Public Library.

PICTURE CREDITS

1. Page 4- Ferrara's Wall. Courtesy of Al Reisz, author.
2. Page 8- Rare snow at Lakefront Airport. Courtesy of Al Reisz, author.
3. Page 9- "The Old Gentilly Road". Artist- Anders Molinari. Public Domain.
4. Page 11- River Deltas. Unknown.
5. Page 15- 'A Louisiana Road'. Public Domain.
6. Page 18 & 19- 'Zero Milestone- San Antonio'. Courtesy of Al Reisz, author.
7. Page 20- 'Elysian Fields Destumping'. Courtesy of Louisiana Division/City Archives, New Orleans Public Library.
8. Page 29- 'Ground Subsidence'. Courtesy of Al Reisz, author.
9. Page 30- 'Naval Air Station'. Courtesy of Louisiana Division/City Archives, New Orleans Public Library.
10. Page 41. Jeff Davis Canal. Courtesy of Louisiana Division/City Archives, New Orleans Public Library.
11 Page 50- Pitt Theater- Unknown.
12. Page 55- Milneburg House. Courtesy of Al Reisz. Author.
13. Page 68- The Hurricane Vine. Courtesy of Al Reisz. Author.
14. Page 69- Andrew Jackson medallion. Unknown.
15. Page 70- Battle of New Orleans. Courtesy of Al Reisz, author.
16. Page 70- Ancient Bayous of N.O. Courtesy of Al Reisz, author.
17. Page 71- Ancient Bayous of N.O. Courtesy of Al Reisz, author.
18. Page 72- Ancient Bayous of N.O. Courtesy of Al Reisz, author.
19. Page 73- Old Portage Sign. Courtesy of Al Reisz, author.

20. Page 74- Historic picture of Lake Pontchartrain shoreline. Courtesy of Louisiana Division/City Archives, New Orleans Public Library.
21. Page 75- Milneburg Lighthouse. Courtesy of Louisiana Division/City Archives, New Orleans Public Library.
22. Page 76- Milneburg camps. Courtesy of Louisiana Division/City Archives, New Orleans Public Library.
23. Page 77- Milneburg Lighthouse. Courtesy of Al Reisz, author.
24. Page 78- Smoky Mary. Unknown.
25. Page 79- Pontchartrain RR timetable. Unknown.
26. Page 80- Elysian Fields. Courtesy of Louisiana Division/City Archives, New Orleans Public Library.
27. Page 81- Verbena Street. Courtesy of Louisiana Division/City Archives, New Orleans Public Library.
28. Page 82- Elysian Fields and Prentiss. Courtesy of Louisiana Division/City Archives, New Orleans Public Library.
29. Page 83- Elysian Fields RR tracks. Courtesy of Louisiana Division/City Archives, New Orleans Public Library.
30. Page 84- Marigny Street. Courtesy of Louisiana Division/City Archives, New Orleans Public Library.
31. Page850- Filmore and Elysian Fields. Courtesy of Louisiana Division/City Archives, New Orleans Public Library.
32. Page 86- Vermillion Street. Courtesy of Louisiana Division/City Archives, New Orleans Public Library.
33. Page 87- New York Street Canal. Courtesy of Louisiana Division/City Archives, New Orleans Public Library.
34. Page 88- I-10 Highrise construction. Courtesy of Louisiana Division/City Archives, New Orleans Public Library.
35. Page 89- London Avenue Canal. Courtesy of Louisiana Division/City Archives, New Orleans Public Library.

36. Page 90- London Avenue Canal, aerial shot. Courtesy of Louisiana Division/City Archives, New Orleans Public Library.
37. Page 91- Aerial shot. Courtesy of Louisiana Division/City Archives, New Orleans Public Library.
38. Page 92- St. Rita's Chapel. Unknown.
39. Page 93- 2nd St. Raphael Church. Unknown.
40. Page 94- 3rd St. Raphael Church. Unknown.
41. Page 95- St. James Major. Courtesy of Al Reisz, author.
42. Page 96- St. Francis Cabrini. Courtesy of Al Reisz, author.
43. Page 97- Pontchartrain Beach Clown. Unknown.
44. Page 125- 'Messina's Sweet Shop'. Courtesy of Al Reisz, author.
45. Page 133- Pelly and the seawall. Courtesy of Al Reisz, author.
46. Page 139- St. Raphael School. Courtesy of Al Reisz, author.
47. Page 140- Lime colored football. Courtesy of Al Reisz, author.
48. Page 176- Spanish Fort. Courtesy of Al Reisz, author.
49. Page 178- Spanish Fort. Courtesy of Al Reisz, author.
50. Page 179- Spanish Fort. Courtesy of Al Reisz, author.
51. Page 180- Spanish Fort. Courtesy of Al Reisz, author.
52. Page 181- Spanish Fort & Bayou St. John. Unknown.
53. Page 182- Spanish Fort. Unknown.
54. Page 183- Milneburg Lighthouse. Courtesy of Al Reisz, author.
55. Page 184- Milneburg Lighthouse. Courtesy of Al Reisz, author.
56. Page 185- Milneburg Lighthouse. Courtesy of Al Reisz, author.
57. Page 186- Milneburg Lighthouse. Courtesy of Al Reisz, author.
58. Page 187- Milneburg Lighthouse. Unknown.

59. Page 188- Shushan Airport. Courtesy of Lakefront Airport.
60. Page 191- Shushan Airport construction. Courtesy of UNO Special Collections.
61. Page 192- Art Deco Terminal Building. Courtesy of Al Reisz, author.
62. Page 193- Fountain of the Four Winds. Courtesy of Al Reisz, author.

Made in the USA
Coppell, TX
31 March 2025

47784683R00115